NLTK Essentials

Build cool NLP and machine learning applications using NLTK and other Python libraries

Nitin Hardeniya

BIRMINGHAM - MUMBAI

NLTK Essentials

First published: July 2015

Production reference: 1220715

Published by Packt Publishing Ltd.
Livery Place
35 Livery Street
Birmingham B3 2PB, UK.

ISBN 978-1-78439-690-9

www.packtpub.com

Credits

Author
Nitin Hardeniya

Reviewers
Afroz Hussain
Sujit Pal
Kumar Raj

Commissioning Editor
Kunal Parikh

Acquisition Editor
Kevin Colaco

Content Development Editor
Samantha Gonsalves

Technical Editor
Rohan Uttam Gosavi

Copy Editors
Neha Vyas
Brandt D'Mello
Samantha Lyon

Project Coordinator
Sanchita Mandal

Proofreader
Safis Editing

Indexer
Mariammal Chettiyar

Graphics
Disha Haria

Production Coordinator
Conidon Miranda

Cover Work
Conidon Miranda

About the Author

Nitin Hardeniya is a data scientist with more than 4 years of experience working with companies such as Fidelity, Groupon, and [24]7-inc. He has worked on a variety of business problems across different domains. He holds a master's degree in computational linguistics from IIIT-H. He is the author of 5 patents in the field of customer experience.

He is passionate about language processing and large unstructured data. He has been using Python for almost 5 years in his day-to-day work. He believes that Python could be a single-point solution to most of the problems related to data science.

He has put on his hacker's hat to write this book and has tried to give you an introduction to all the sophisticated tools related to NLP and machine learning in a very simplified form. In this book, he has also provided a workaround using some of the amazing capabilities of Python libraries, such as NLTK, scikit-learn, pandas, and NumPy.

About the Reviewers

Afroz Hussain is a data scientist by profession and is currently associated with a US-based data science and ML start-up, PredictifyMe. He has experience of working on many data science projects and has extensive experience of Python, scikit-learn, and text mining with NLTK. He has more than 10 years of programming and software development experience along with the experience of working on data analysis and business intelligence projects. He has acquired new skills in data science by taking online courses and taking part in Kaggle competitions.

Sujit Pal works at Elsevier Labs, which is a research and development group within the Reed-Elsevier PLC group. His interests are in the fields of information retrieval, distributed processing, ontology development, natural language processing, and machine learning. He is also interested in and writes code in Python, Scala, and Java. He combines his skills in these areas in order to help build new features or feature improvements for different products across the company. He believes in lifelong learning and blogs about his experiences at `sujitpal.blogspot.com`.

Kumar Raj serves as a data scientist II at Hewlett-Packard Software solutions in the research and development department, where he is responsible for developing the analytics layer for core HP software products. He is a graduate from Indian Institute of Technology, Kharagpur, and has more than 2 years of experience in various big data analytics domains, namely text analytics, web crawling and scraping, HR analytics, virtualization system performance optimization, and climate change forecasting.

www.PacktPub.com

Support files, eBooks, discount offers, and more

For support files and downloads related to your book, please visit `www.PacktPub.com`.

Did you know that Packt offers eBook versions of every book published, with PDF and ePub files available? You can upgrade to the eBook version at `www.PacktPub.com` and as a print book customer, you are entitled to a discount on the eBook copy. Get in touch with us at `service@packtpub.com` for more details.

At `www.PacktPub.com`, you can also read a collection of free technical articles, sign up for a range of free newsletters and receive exclusive discounts and offers on Packt books and eBooks.

`https://www2.packtpub.com/books/subscription/packtlib`

Do you need instant solutions to your IT questions? PacktLib is Packt's online digital book library. Here, you can search, access, and read Packt's entire library of books.

Why subscribe?

- Fully searchable across every book published by Packt
- Copy and paste, print, and bookmark content
- On demand and accessible via a web browser

Free access for Packt account holders

If you have an account with Packt at `www.PacktPub.com`, you can use this to access PacktLib today and view 9 entirely free books. Simply use your login credentials for immediate access.

Table of Contents

Preface

This book is about NLTK and how NLTK can be used in conjunction with other Python libraries. NLTK is one of the most popular and widely used libraries in the natural language processing (NLP) community. The beauty of NLTK lies in its simplicity, where most of the complex NLP tasks can be implemented by using a few lines of code.

The first half of this book starts with an introduction to Python and NLP. In this book, you'll learn a few generic preprocessing techniques, such as tokenization, stemming, and stop word removal, and some NLP-specific preprocessing, such as POS tagging and NER that are involved in most text-related NLP tasks. We gradually move on to more complex NLP tasks, such as parsing and other NLP applications.

The second half of this book focuses more on how some of the NLP applications, such as text classification, can be deployed using NLTK and scikit-learn. We talk about some other Python libraries that you should know about for text-mining-related or NLP-related tasks. We also look at data gathering from the Web and social media and how NLTK can be used on a large scale in this chapter.

What this book covers

Chapter 1, Introduction to Natural Language Processing, talks about some of the basic concepts in NLP and introduces you to NLTK and Python. This chapter focuses on getting you up to speed with NLTK and how to start with the installation of the required libraries to build one very basic word cloud example.

Chapter 2, Text Wrangling and Cleansing, talks about all the preprocessing steps required in any text mining/NLP task. In this chapter, we discuss tokenization, stemming, stop word removal, and other text cleansing processes in detail and how easy it is to implement these in NLTK.

Chapter 3, Part of Speech Tagging, focuses on giving you an overview of POS tagging. In this chapter, you will also see how to apply some of these taggers using NLTK and we will talk about the different NLP taggers available in NLTK.

Chapter 4, Parsing Structure in Text, moves deep in NLP. It talks about different parsing methods and how it can be implemented using NLTK. It talks about the importance of parsing in the context of NLP and some of the common information extraction techniques, such as entity extraction.

Chapter 5, NLP Applications, talks about different NLP applications. This chapter will help you build one simple NLP application using some of the knowledge you've assimilated so far.

Chapter 6, Text Classification, describes some of the common classification techniques in machine learning. This chapter mainly focuses on a text corpus and how to build a pipeline to implement a text classifier using NLTK and scikit. We also talk about text clustering and topic modeling.

Chapter 7, Web Crawling, deals with the other aspects of NLP, data science, and data gathering and talks about how to get the data from one of the biggest sources of text data, which is the Web. We will learn to build a good crawler using the Python library, Scrapy.

Chapter 8, Using NLTK with Other Python Libraries, talks about some of the backbone Python libraries, such as NumPy and SciPy. It also gives you a brief introduction to pandas for data processing and matplotlib for visualization.

Chapter 9, Social Media Mining in Python, is dedicated to data collection. Here, we talk about social media and other problems related to social media. We also discuss the aspects of how to gather, analyze, and visualize data from social media.

Chapter 10, Text Mining at Scale, talks about how we can scale NLTK and some other Python libraries to perform at scale in the era of big data. We give a brief over view of how NLTK and scikit can be used with Hadoop.

What you need for this book

We need the following software for this book:

Chapter number	Software required (with version)	Free/ Proprietary	Download links to the software	Hardware specifications	OS required

1-5	Python/ Anaconda
	NLTK
		Free	`https://www.python.org/`
			`http://continuum.io/downloads`
			`http://www.nltk.org/`
				Common Unix Printing System	any

6	scikit-learn and gensim	Free	`http://scikit-learn.org/stable/` `https://radimrehurek.com/gensim/`	Common Unix Printing System	any
7	Scrapy	Free	`http://scrapy.org/`	Common Unix Printing System	any

8	NumPy, SciPy, pandas, and matplotlib	Free	`http://www.numpy.org/`
			`http://www.scipy.org/`
			`http://pandas.pydata.org/`
			`http://matplotlib.org/`
				Common Unix Printing System	any

9	Twitter Python APIs and Facebook Python APIs	Free	`https://dev.twitter.com/overview/api/twitter-libraries` `https://developers.facebook.com`	Common Unix Printing System	any

Who this book is for

If you are an NLP or machine learning enthusiast with some or no experience in text processing, then this book is for you. This book is also ideal for expert Python programmers who want to learn NLTK quickly.

Conventions

In this book, you will find a number of text styles that distinguish between different kinds of information. Here are some examples of these styles and an explanation of their meaning.

Code words in text, database table names, folder names, filenames, file extensions, pathnames, dummy URLs, user input, and Twitter handles are shown as follows: "We need to create a file named `NewsSpider.py` and put it in the path `/tutorial/spiders`."

A Python block of code is set as follows:

```
>>>import nltk
>>>import numpy
```

A Hive block of code is set as follows:

```
add FILE vectorizer.pkl;
add FILE classifier.pkl;
```

In *chapter 7, Web Crawling,* we have used a IPython notation for Scrapy shell

```
In [1] : sel.xpath('//title/text()')
Out[1]: [<Selector xpath='//title/text()' data=u' Google News'>]
```

Any command-line input or output is written as follows:

```
# cp /usr/src/asterisk-addons/configs/cdr_mysql.conf.sample
     /etc/asterisk/cdr_mysql.conf
```

Warnings or important notes appear in a box like this.

Tips and tricks appear like this.

Reader feedback

Feedback from our readers is always welcome. Let us know what you think about this book—what you liked or disliked. Reader feedback is important for us as it helps us develop titles that you will really get the most out of.

To send us general feedback, simply e-mail `feedback@packtpub.com`, and mention the book's title in the subject of your message.

If there is a topic that you have expertise in and you are interested in either writing or contributing to a book, see our author guide at `www.packtpub.com/authors`.

Customer support

Now that you are the proud owner of a Packt book, we have a number of things to help you to get the most from your purchase.

Downloading the example code

You can download the example code files from your account at `http://www.packtpub.com` for all the Packt Publishing books you have purchased. If you purchased this book elsewhere, you can visit `http://www.packtpub.com/support` and register to have the files e-mailed directly to you.

Errata

Although we have taken every care to ensure the accuracy of our content, mistakes do happen. If you find a mistake in one of our books—maybe a mistake in the text or the code—we would be grateful if you could report this to us. By doing so, you can save other readers from frustration and help us improve subsequent versions of this book. If you find any errata, please report them by visiting `http://www.packtpub.com/submit-errata`, selecting your book, clicking on the **Errata Submission Form** link, and entering the details of your errata. Once your errata are verified, your submission will be accepted and the errata will be uploaded to our website or added to any list of existing errata under the Errata section of that title.

To view the previously submitted errata, go to `https://www.packtpub.com/books/content/support` and enter the name of the book in the search field. The required information will appear under the **Errata** section.

Piracy

Piracy of copyrighted material on the Internet is an ongoing problem across all media. At Packt, we take the protection of our copyright and licenses very seriously. If you come across any illegal copies of our works in any form on the Internet, please provide us with the location address or website name immediately so that we can pursue a remedy.

Please contact us at `copyright@packtpub.com` with a link to the suspected pirated material.

We appreciate your help in protecting our authors and our ability to bring you valuable content.

Questions

If you have a problem with any aspect of this book, you can contact us at `questions@packtpub.com`, and we will do our best to address the problem.

1

Introduction to Natural Language Processing

I will start with the introduction to **Natural Language Processing** (**NLP**). Language is a central part of our day to day life, and it's so interesting to work on any problem related to languages. I hope this book will give you a flavor of NLP, will motivate you to learn some amazing concepts of NLP, and will inspire you to work on some of the challenging NLP applications.

In my own language, the study of language processing is called NLP. People who are deeply involved in the study of language are linguists, while the term 'computational linguist' applies to the study of processing languages with the application of computation. Essentially, a computational linguist will be a computer scientist who has enough understanding of languages, and can apply his computational skills to model different aspects of the language. While computational linguists address the theoretical aspect of language, NLP is nothing but the application of computational linguistics.

NLP is more about the application of computers on different language nuances, and building real-world applications using NLP techniques. In a practical context, NLP is analogous to teaching a language to a child. Some of the most common tasks like understanding words, sentences, and forming grammatically and structurally correct sentences, are very natural to humans. In NLP, some of these tasks translate to tokenization, chunking, part of speech tagging, parsing, machine translation, speech recognition, and most of them are still the toughest challenges for computers. I will be talking more on the practical side of NLP, assuming that we all have some background in NLP. The expectation for the reader is to have minimal understanding of any programming language and an interest in NLP and Language.

By end of the chapter we want readers

- A brief introduction to NLP and related concepts.

- Install Python, NLTK and other libraries.
- Write some very basic Python and NLTK code snippets.

If you have never heard the term NLP, then please take some time to read any of the books mentioned here—just for an initial few chapters. A quick reading of at least the Wikipedia page relating to NLP is a must:

- *Speech and Language Processing* by Daniel Jurafsky and James H. Martin
- *Statistical Natural Language Processing* by Christopher D. Manning and Hinrich Schütze

Why learn NLP?

I start my discussion with the Gartner's new hype cycle and you can clearly see NLP on top of the cycle. Currently, NLP is one of the rarest skill sets that is required in the industry. After the advent of big data, the major challenge is that we need more people who are good with not just structured, but also with semi or unstructured data. We are generating **petabytes** of Weblogs, tweets, Facebook feeds, chats, e-mails, and reviews. Companies are collecting all these different kind of data for better customer targeting and meaningful insights. To process all these unstructured data source we need people who understand NLP.

We are in the age of information; we can't even imagine our life without Google. We use Siri for the most of basic stuff. We use spam filters for filtering spam emails. We need spell checker on our Word document. There are many examples of real world NLP applications around us.

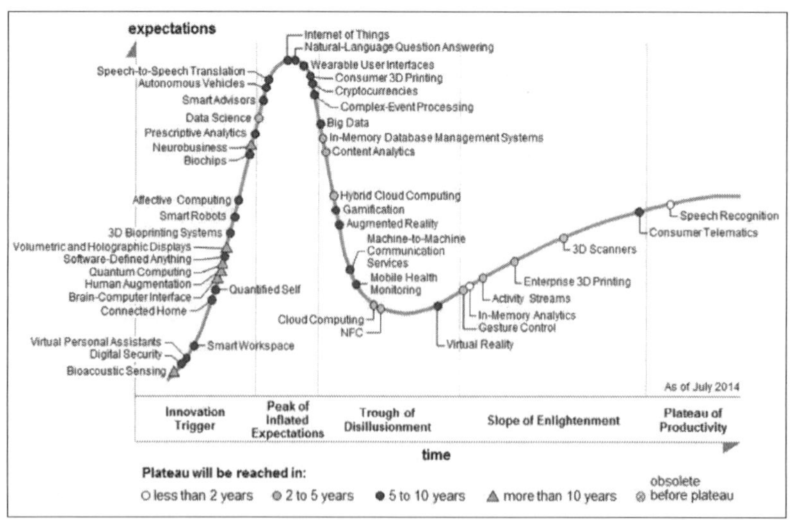

Image is taken from `http://www.gartner.com/newsroom/id/2819918`

Let me also give you some examples of the amazing NLP applications that you can use, but are not aware that they are built on NLP:

- Spell correction (MS Word/ any other editor)
- Search engines (Google, Bing, Yahoo, wolframalpha)
- Speech engines (Siri, Google Voice)
- Spam classifiers (All e-mail services)
- News feeds (Google, Yahoo!, and so on)
- Machine translation (Google Translate, and so on)
- IBM Watson

Building these applications requires a very specific skill set with a great understanding of language and tools to process the language efficiently. So it's not just hype that makes NLP one of the most niche areas, but it's the kind of application that can be created using NLP that makes it one of the most unique skills to have.

To achieve some of the above applications and other basic NLP preprocessing, there are many open source tools available. Some of them are developed by organizations to build their own NLP applications, while some of them are open-sourced. Here is a small list of available NLP tools:

- GATE
- Mallet
- Open NLP
- UIMA
- Stanford toolkit
- Genism
- **Natural Language Tool Kit (NLTK)**

Most of the tools are written in Java and have similar functionalities. Some of them are robust and have a different variety of NLP tools available. However, when it comes to the ease of use and explanation of the concepts, NLTK scores really high. NLTK is also a very good learning kit because the learning curve of Python (on which NLTK is written) is very fast. NLTK has incorporated most of the NLP tasks, it's very elegant and easy to work with. For all these reasons, NLTK has become one of the most popular libraries in the NLP community:

I am assuming all you guys know Python. If not, I urge you to learn Python. There are many basic tutorials on Python available online. There are lots of books also available that give you a quick overview of the language. We will also look into some of the features of Python, while going through the different topics. But for now, even if you only know the basics of Python, such as lists, strings, regular expressions, and basic I/O, you should be good to go.

Python can be installed from the following website:

`https://www.python.org/downloads/`

`http://continuum.io/downloads`

`https://store.enthought.com/downloads/`

I would recommend using Anaconda or Canopy Python distributions. The reason being that these distributions come with bundled libraries, such as `scipy`, `numpy`, `scikit`, and so on, which are used for data analysis and other applications related to NLP and related fields. Even NLTK is part of this distribution.

Please follow the instructions and install NLTK and NLTK data:

`http://www.nltk.org/install.html`

Let's test everything.

Open the terminal on your respective operating systems. Then run:

```
$ python
```

This should open the Python interpreter:

```
Python 2.6.6 (r266:84292, Oct 15 2013, 07:32:41)
[GCC 4.4.7 20120313 (Red Hat 4.4.7-4)] on linux2
Type "help", "copyright", "credits" or "license" for more information.
>>>
```

I hope you got a similar looking output here. There is a chance that you will have received a different looking output, but ideally you will get the latest version of Python (I recommend that to be 2.7), the compiler GCC, and the operating system details. I know the latest version of Python will be in 3.0+ range, but as with any other open source systems, we should tries to hold back to a more stable version as opposed to jumping on to the latest version. If you have moved to Python 3.0+, please have a look at the link below to gain an understanding about what new features have been added:

`https://docs.python.org/3/whatsnew/3.4.html.`

UNIX based systems will have Python as a default program. Windows users can set the path to get Python working. Let's check whether we have installed NLTK correctly:

```
>>>import nltk
>>>print "Python and NLTK installed successfully"
Python and NLTK installed successfully
```

Hey, we are good to go!

Let's start playing with Python!

We'll not be diving too deep into Python; however, we'll give you a quick tour of Python essentials. Still, I think for the benefit of the audience, we should have a quick five minute tour. We'll talk about the basics of data structures, some frequently used functions, and the general construct of Python in the next few sections.

I highly recommend the two hour Google Python class. `https://developers.google.com/edu/python` should be good enough to start. Please go through the Python website `https://www.python.org/` for more tutorials and other resources.

Lists

Lists are one of the most commonly used data structures in Python. They are pretty much comparable to arrays in other programming languages. Let's start with some of the most important functions that a Python list provide.

Try the following in the Python console:

```
>>> lst=[1,2,3,4]
>>> # mostly like arrays in typical languages
>>>print lst
[1, 2, 3, 4]
```

Python lists can be accessed using much more flexible indexing. Here are some examples:

```
>>>print 'First element' +lst[0]
```

You will get an error message like this:

```
TypeError: cannot concatenate 'str' and 'int' objects
```

The reason being that Python is an interpreted language, and checks for the type of the variables at the time it evaluates the expression. We need not initialize and declare the type of variable at the time of declaration. Our list has integer object and cannot be concatenated as a print function. It will only accept a string object. For this reason, we need to convert list elements to string. The process is also known as type casting.

```
>>>print 'First element :' +str(lst[0])
>>>print 'last element :' +str(lst[-1])
>>>print 'first three elements :' +str(lst[0:2])
>>>print 'last three elements :'+str(lst[-3:])
First element :1
last element :4
first three elements :[1, 2,3]
last three elements :[2, 3, 4]
```

Helping yourself

The best way to learn more about different data types and functions is to use help functions like `help()` and `dir(lst)`.

The `dir(python object)` command is used to list all the given attributes of the given Python object. Like if you pass a list object, it will list all the cool things you can do with lists:

```
>>>dir(lst)
>>>' , '.join(dir(lst))
'__add__ , __class__ , __contains__ , __delattr__ , __delitem__ , __delslice__ , __doc__ , __eq__ , __format__ , __ge__ , __getattribute__ , __getitem__ , __getslice__ , __gt__ , __hash__ , __iadd__ , __imul__ , __init__ , __iter__ , __le__ , __len__ , __lt__ , __mul__ , __ne__ , __new__ , __reduce__ , __reduce_ex__ , __repr__ , __reversed__ , __rmul__ , __setattr__ , __setitem__ , __setslice__ , __sizeof__ , __str__ , __subclasshook__ , append , count , extend , index , insert , pop , remove , reverse , sort'
```

With the `help(python object)` command, we can get detailed documentation for the given Python object, and also give a few examples of how to use the Python object:

```
>>>help(lst.index)
Help on built-in function index:
```

```
index(...)
    L.index(value, [start, [stop]]) -> integer -- return first index of
value.
This function raises a ValueError if the value is not present.
```

So `help` and `dir` can be used on any Python data type, and are a very nice way to learn about the function and other details of that object. It also provides you with some basic examples to work with, which I found useful in most cases.

Strings in Python are very similar to other languages, but the manipulation of strings is one of the main features of Python. It's immensely easy to work with strings in Python. Even something very simple, like splitting a string, takes effort in Java / C, while you will see how easy it is in Python.

Using the help function that we used previously, you can get help for any Python object and any function. Let's have some more examples with the other most commonly used data type strings:

- **Split**: This is a method to split the string based on some delimiters. If no argument is provided it assumes whitespace as delimiter.

  ```
  >>> mystring="Monty Python !  And the holy Grail ! \n"
  >>> print mystring.split()
  ['Monty', 'Python', '!', 'and', 'the', 'holy', 'Grail', '!']
  ```

- **Strip**: This is a method that can remove trailing whitespace, like '\n', '\n\r' from the string:

  ```
  >>> print mystring.strip()
  >>>Monty Python !  and the holy Grail !
  ```

  If you notice the '\n' character is stripped off. There are also methods like `rstrip()` and `lstrip()` to strip trailing whitespaces to the right and left of the string.

- **Upper/Lower**: We can change the case of the string using these methods:

  ```
  >>> print (mystring.upper()
  >>>MONTY PYTHON !AND THE HOLY GRAIL !
  ```

- **Replace**: This will help you substitute a substring from the string:

```
>>> print mystring.replace('!','''''')
>>> Monty Python   and the holy Grail
```

There are tons of string functions. I have just talked about some of the most frequently used.

Please look the following link for more functions and examples: https://docs.python.org/2/library/string.html.

Regular expressions

One other important skill for an NLP enthusiast is working with regular expression. Regular expression is effectively pattern matching on strings. We heavily use pattern extrication to get meaningful information from large amounts of messy text data. The following are all the regular expressions you need. I haven't used any regular expressions beyond these in my entire life:

- `(a period)`: This expression matches any single character except newline `\n`.
- `\w`: This expression will match a character or a digit equivalent to [a-z A-Z 0-9]
- \W (*upper case W*) matches any non-word character.
- `\s`: This expression (*lowercase s*) matches a single whitespace character - space, newline, return, tab, form [`\n\r\t\f`].
- `\S`: This expression matches any non-whitespace character.
- `\t`: This expression performs a tab operation.
- `\n`: This expression is used for a newline character.
- `\r`: This expression is used for a return character.
- `\d`: Decimal digit [0-9].
- `^`: This expression is used at the start of the string.
- `$`: This expression is used at the end of the string.
- `\`: This expression is used to nullify the specialness of the special character. For example, you want to match the `$` symbol, then add `\` in front of it.

Let's search for something in the running example, where `mystring` is the same string object, and we will try to look for some patterns in that. A substring search is one of the common use-cases of the `re` module. Let's implement this:

```
>>># We have to import re module to use regular expression
>>>import re
>>>if re.search('Python',mystring):
>>>    print "We found python "
>>>else:
>>>    print "NO "
```

Once this is executed, we get the message as follows:

```
We found python
```

We can do more pattern finding using regular expressions. One of the common functions that is used in finding all the patterns in a string is `findall`. It will look for the given patterns in the string, and will give you a list of all the matched objects:

```
>>>import re
>>>print re.findall('!',mystring)
['!', '!']
```

As we can see there were two instances of the `"!"` in the `mystring` and `findall` return both object as a list.

Dictionaries

The other most commonly used data structure is dictionaries, also known as **associative arrays/memories** in other programming languages. Dictionaries are data structures that are indexed by keys, which can be any immutable type; such as strings and numbers can always be keys.

Dictionaries are handy data structure that used widely across programming languages to implement many algorithms. Python dictionaries are one of the most elegant implementations of hash tables in any programming language. It's so easy to work around dictionary, and the great thing is that with few nuggets of code you can build a very complex data structure, while the same task can take so much time and coding effort in other languages. This gives the programmer more time to focus on algorithms rather than the data structure itself.

I am using one of the very common use cases of dictionaries to get the frequency distribution of words in a given text. With just few lines of the following code, you can get the frequency of words. Just try the same task in any other language and you will understand how amazing Python is:

```
>>># declare a dictionary
>>>word_freq={}
>>>for tok in string.split():
>>>    if tok in word_freq:
>>>        word_freq [tok]+=1
>>>    else:
>>>        word_freq [tok]=1
>>>print word_freq
{'!': 2, 'and': 1, 'holy': 1, 'Python': 1, 'Grail': 1, 'the': 1, 'Monty':
1}
```

Writing functions

As any other programming langauge Python also has its way of writing functions. Function in Python start with keyword `def` followed by the function name and parentheses `()`. Similar to any other programming language any arguments and the type of the argument should be placed within these parentheses. The actual code starts with `(:) colon symbol`. The initial lines of the code are typically doc string (comments), then we have code body and function ends with a return statement. For example in the given example the function `wordfreq` start with `def` keyword, there is no argument to this function and the function ends with a return statement.

```
>>>import sys
>>>def wordfreq (mystring):
>>>    '''
>>>    Function to generated the frequency distribution of the given text
>>>    '''
>>>    print mystring
>>>    word_freq={}
>>>    for tok in mystring.split():
>>>        if tok in word_freq:
>>>            word_freq [tok]+=1
>>>        else:
>>>            word_freq [tok]=1
```

```
>>>     print word_freq
>>>def main():
>>>     str="This is my fist python program"
>>>     wordfreq(str)
>>>if __name__ == '__main__':
>>>     main()
```

This was the same code that we wrote in the previous section the idea of writing in a form of function is to make the code re-usable and readable. The interpreter style of writing Python is also very common but for writing big programes it will be a good practice to use function/classes and one of the programming paradigm. We also wanted the user to write and run first Python program. You need to follow these steps to achive this.

1. Open an empty python file `mywordfreq.py` in your prefered text editor.
2. Write/Copy the code above in the code snippet to the file.
3. Open the command prompt in your Operating system.
4. Run following command prompt:

   ```
   $ python mywordfreq,py "This is my fist python program !!"
   ```

5. Output should be:

   ```
   {'This': 1, 'is': 1, 'python': 1, 'fist': 1, 'program': 1, 'my':
   1}
   ```

Now you have a very basic understanding about some common data-structures that python provides. You can write a full Python program and able to run that. I think this is good enough I think with this much of an introduction to Python you can manage for the initial chapters.

Please have a look at some Python tutorials on the following website to learn more commands on Python:

`https://wiki.python.org/moin/BeginnersGuide`

Diving into NLTK

Instead of going further into the theoretical aspects of natural language processing, let's start with a quick dive into NLTK. I am going to start with some basic example use cases of NLTK. There is a good chance that you have already done something similar. First, I will give a typical Python programmer approach, and then move on to NLTK for a much more efficient, robust, and clean solution.

We will start analyzing with some example text content. For the current example, I have taken the content from Python's home page.

```
>>>import urllib2
>>># urllib2 is use to download the html content of the web link
>>>response = urllib2.urlopen('http://python.org/')
>>># You can read the entire content of a file using read() method
>>>html = response.read()
>>>print len(html)
47020
```

We don't have any clue about the kind of topics that are discussed in this URL, so let's start with an **exploratory data analysis (EDA)**. Typically in a text domain, EDA can have many meanings, but will go with a simple case of what kinds of terms dominate the document. What are the topics? How frequent they are? The process will involve some level of preprocessing steps. We will try to do this first in a pure Python way, and then we will do it using NLTK.

Let's start with cleaning the html tags. One ways to do this is to select just the `tokens`, including numbers and character. Anybody who has worked with regular expression should be able to convert html string into list of `tokens`:

```
>>># Regular expression based split the string
>>>tokens = [tok for tok in html.split()]
>>>print "Total no of tokens :"+ str(len(tokens))
>>># First 100 tokens
>>>print tokens[0:100]
Total no of tokens :2860
['<!doctype', 'html>', '<!--[if', 'lt', 'IE', '7]>', '<html', 'class="no-
js', 'ie6', 'lt-ie7', 'lt-ie8', 'lt-ie9">', '<![endif]-->', '<!--[if',
'IE', '7]>', '<html', 'class="no-js', 'ie7', 'lt-ie8', 'lt-ie9">',
'<![endif]-->', ''type="text/css"', 'media="not', 'print,', 'braille,'
...]
```

As you can see, there is an excess of html tags and other unwanted characters when we use the preceding method. A cleaner version of the same task will look something like this:

```
>>>import re
>>># using the split function
>>>#https://docs.python.org/2/library/re.html
>>>tokens = re.split('\W+',html)
```

```
>>>print len(tokens)
>>>print tokens[0:100]
5787
['', 'doctype', 'html', 'if', 'lt', 'IE', '7', 'html', 'class', 'no',
'js', 'ie6', 'lt', 'ie7', 'lt', 'ie8', 'lt', 'ie9', 'endif', 'if',
'IE', '7', 'html', 'class', 'no', 'js', 'ie7', 'lt', 'ie8', 'lt', 'ie9',
'endif', 'if', 'IE', '8', 'msapplication', 'tooltip', 'content', 'The',
'official', 'home', 'of', 'the', 'Python', 'Programming', 'Language',
'meta', 'name', 'apple' ...]
```

This looks much cleaner now. But still you can do more; I leave it to you to try to remove as much noise as you can. You can clean some HTML tags that are still popping up, You probably also want to look for word length as a criteria and remove words that have a length one—it will remove elements like `7`, `8`, and so on, which are just noise in this case. Now instead writing some of these preprocessing steps from scratch let's move to NLTK for the same task. There is a function called `clean_html()` that can do all the cleaning that we were looking for:

```
>>>import nltk
>>># http://www.nltk.org/api/nltk.html#nltk.util.clean_html
>>>clean = nltk.clean_html(html)
>>># clean will have entire string removing all the html noise
>>>tokens = [tok for tok in clean.split()]
>>>print tokens[:100]
['Welcome', 'to', 'Python.org', 'Skip', 'to', 'content', '&#9660;',
'Close', 'Python', 'PSF', 'Docs', 'PyPI', 'Jobs', 'Community', '&#9650;',
'The', 'Python', 'Network', '&equiv;', 'Menu', 'Arts', 'Business' ...]
```

Cool, right? This definitely is much cleaner and easier to do.

Let's try to get the frequency distribution of these terms. First, let's do it the Pure Python way, then I will tell you the NLTK recipe.

```
>>>import operator
>>>freq_dis={}
>>>for tok in tokens:
>>>    if tok in freq_dis:
>>>        freq_dis[tok]+=1
>>>    else:
>>>        freq_dis[tok]=1
>>># We want to sort this dictionary on values ( freq in this case )
```

```
>>>sorted_freq_dist= sorted(freq_dis.items(), key=operator.itemgetter(1), reverse=True)
>>> print sorted_freq_dist[:25]
[('Python', 55), ('>>>', 23), ('and', 21), ('to', 18), (',', 18), ('the', 14), ('of', 13), ('for', 12), ('a', 11), ('Events', 11), ('News', 11), ('is', 10), ('2014-', 10), ('More', 9), ('#', 9), ('3', 9), ('=', 8), ('in', 8), ('with', 8), ('Community', 7), ('The', 7), ('Docs', 6), ('Software', 6), (':', 6), ('3:', 5), ('that', 5), ('sum', 5)]
```

Naturally, as this is Python's home page, Python and the `(>>>)` interpreter symbol are the most common terms, also giving a sense of the website.

A better and more efficient approach is to use NLTK's `FreqDist()` function. For this, we will take a look at the same code we developed before:

```
>>>import nltk
>>>Freq_dist_nltk=nltk.FreqDist(tokens)
>>>print Freq_dist_nltk
>>>for k,v in Freq_dist_nltk.items():
>>>     print str(k)+':'+str(v)
<FreqDist: 'Python': 55, '>>>': 23, 'and': 21, ',': 18, 'to': 18, 'the': 14, 'of': 13, 'for': 12, 'Events': 11, 'News': 11, ...>
Python:55
>>>:23
and:21
,:18
to:18
the:14
of:13
for:12
Events:11
News:11
```

Downloading the example code

You can download the example code files from your account at `http://www.packtpub.com` for all the Packt Publishing books you have purchased. If you purchased this book elsewhere, you can visit `http://www.packtpub.com/support` and register to have the files e-mailed directly to you.

Let's now do some more funky things. Let's plot this:

```
>>>Freq_dist_nltk.plot(50, cumulative=False)
>>># below is the plot for the frequency distributions
```

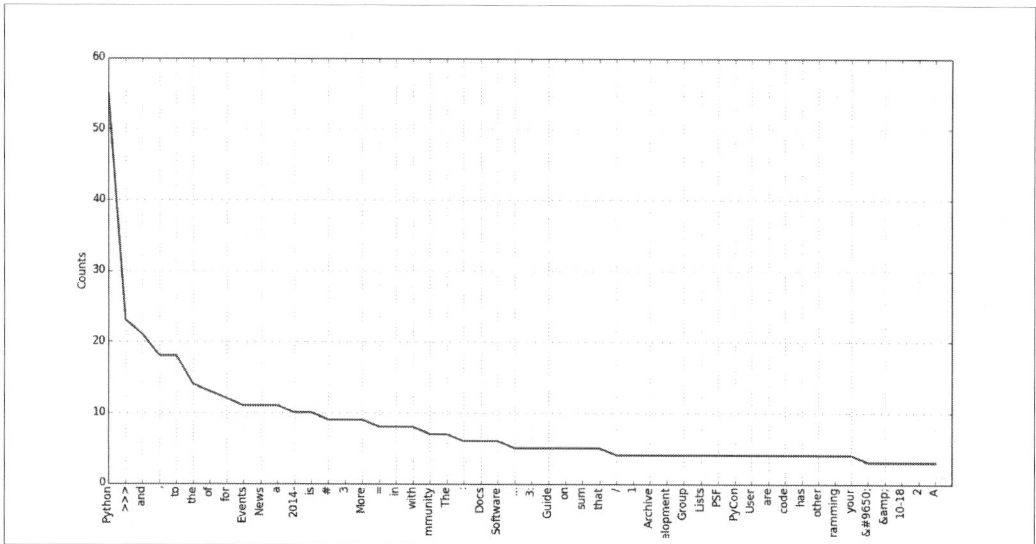

We can see that the cumulative frequency is growing, and at some point the curve is going into long tail. Still, there is some noise, there are words like `the`, `of`, `for`, and `=`. These are useless words, and there is a terminology for them. These words are stop words; words like `the`, `a`, `an`, and so on. Article pronouns are generally present in most of the documents, hence they are not discriminative enough to be informative. In most of the NLP and information retrieval tasks, people generally remove stop words. Let's go back again to our running example:

```
>>>stopwords=[word.strip().lower() for word in open("PATH/english.stop.
txt")]
>>>clean_tokens=[tok for tok in tokens if len(tok.lower())>1 and (tok.
lower() not in stopwords)]
```

```
>>>Freq_dist_nltk=nltk.FreqDist(clean_tokens)
>>>Freq_dist_nltk.plot(50, cumulative=False)
```

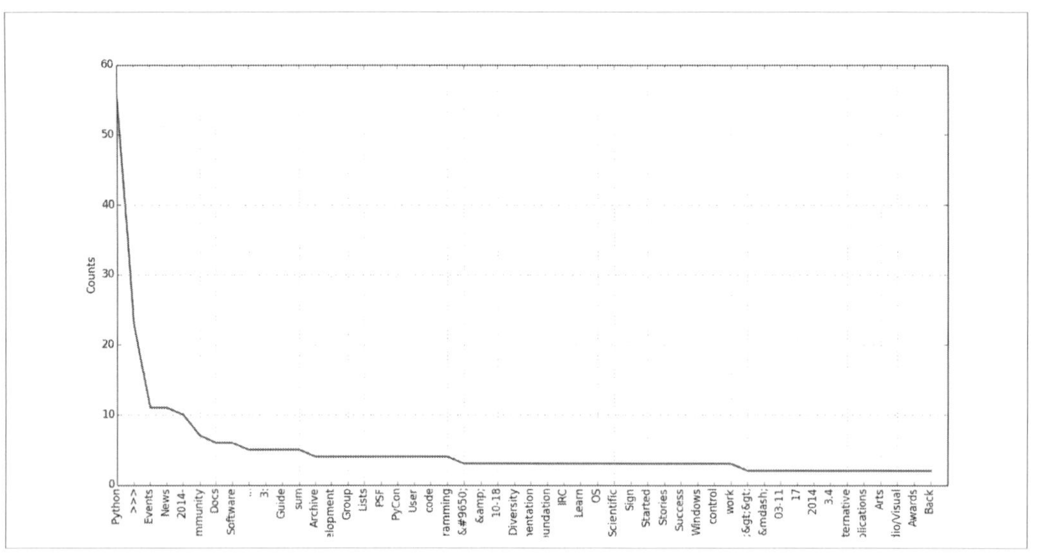

Please go to `http://www.wordle.net/advanced` for more word clouds.

Looks much cleaner now! After finishing this much, you can go to **wordle** and put the distribution in a form of a CSV and you should be able to get something like this word cloud:

Your turn

- Please try the same exercise for different URLs.
- Try to reach the word cloud.

Summary

To summarize, this chapter was intended to give you a brief introduction to Natural Language Processing. The book does assume some background in NLP and programming in Python, but we have tried to give a very quick head start to Python and NLP. We have installed all the related packages that are require for us to work with NLTK. We wanted to give you, with a few simple lines of code, an idea of how to use NLTK. We were able to deliver an amazing word cloud, which is a great way of visualizing the topics in a large amount of unstructured text, and is quite popular in the industry for text analytics. I think the goal was to set up everything around NLTK, and to get Python working smoothly on your system. You should also be able to write and run basic Python programs. I wanted the reader to feel the power of the NLTK library, and build a small running example that will involve a basic application around word cloud. If the reader is able to generate the word cloud, I think we were successful.

In the next few chapters, we will learn more about Python as a language, and its features related to process natural language. We will explore some of the basic NLP preprocessing steps and learn about some of basic concepts related to NLP.

2

Text Wrangling and Cleansing

The previous chapter was all about you getting a head start on Python as well as **NLTK**. We learned about how we can start some meaningful **EDA** with any corpus of text. We did all the pre-processing part in a very crude and simple manner.
In this chapter, will go over preprocessing steps like **tokenization**, **stemming**, **lemmatization**, and **stop word** removal in more detail. We will explore all the tools in NLTK for text wrangling. We will talk about all the pre-processing steps used in modern NLP applications, the different ways to achieve some of these tasks, as well as the general do's and don'ts. The idea is to give you enough information about these tools so that you can decide what kind of pre-processing tool you need for your application. By the end of this chapter, readers should know :

- About all the data wrangling, and to perform it using NLTK
- What is the importance of text cleansing and what are the common tasks that can be achieved using NLTK

What is text wrangling?

It's really hard to define the term text/data wrangling. I will define it as all the pre-processing and all the heavy lifting you do before you have a machine readable and formatted text from raw data. The process involves **data munging**, **text cleansing**, **specific preprocessing**, **tokenization**, **stemming** or **lemmatization** and **stop word removal**. Let's start with a basic example of parsing a `csv` file:

```
>>>import csv
>>>with open('example.csv','rb')  as f:
>>>     reader = csv.reader(f,delimiter=',',quotechar='"')
>>>     for line in reader :
>>>         print line[1]    # assuming the second field is the raw sting
```

Here we are trying to parse a `csv`, in above code line will be a list of all the column elements of the `csv`. We can customize this to work on any delimiter and quoting character. Now once we have the raw string, we can apply different kinds of text wrangling that we learned in the last chapter. The point here is to equip you with enough detail to deal with any day to day `csv` files.

A clear process flow for some of the most commonly accepted document types is shown in the following block diagram:

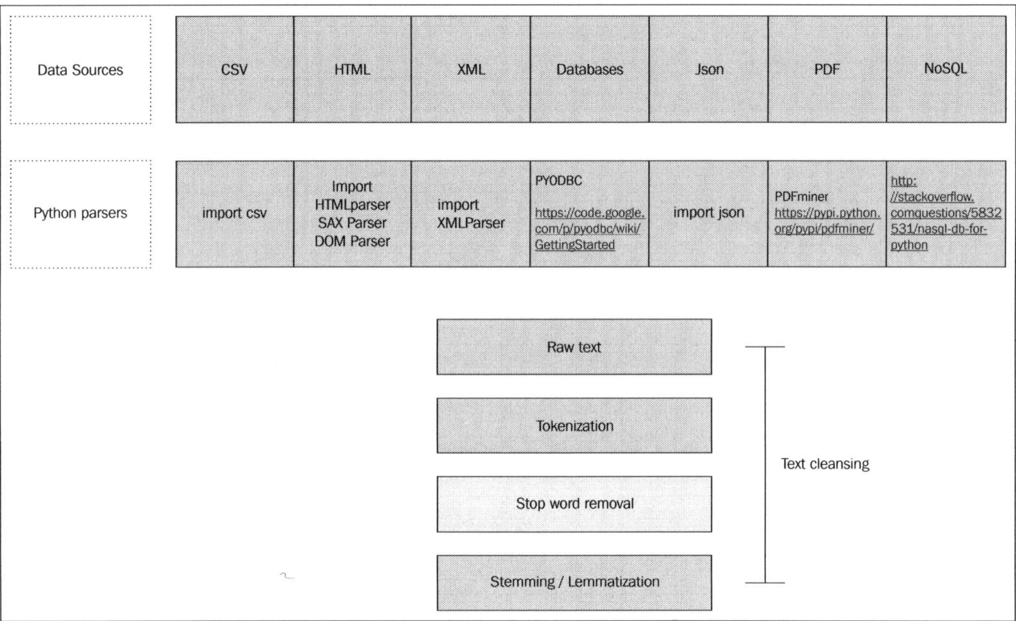

I have listed most common data sources in the first stack of the diagram. In most cases, the data will be residing in one of these data formats. In the next step, I have listed the most commonly used Python wrappers around those data formats. For example, in the case of a `csv` file, Python's `csv` module is the most robust way of handling the `csv` file. It allows you to play with different splitters, different quote characters, and so on.

The other most commonly used files are `json`.

For example, `json` looks like:

```
{
  "array": [1,2,3,4],
 "boolean": True,
  "object": {
    "a": "b"
  },
  "string": "Hello World"
}
```

Let's say we want to process the string. The parsing code will be:

```
>>>import json
>>>jsonfile = open('example.json')
>>>data = json.load(jsonfile)
>>>print data['string']
"Hello World"
```

We are just loading a `json` file using the `json` module. Python allows you to choose and process it to a raw string form. Please have a look at the diagram to get more details about all the data sources, and their parsing packages in Python. I have only given pointers here; please feel free to search the web for more details about these packages.

So before you write your own parser to parse these different document formats, please have a look at the second row for available parsers in Python. Once you reach a raw string, all the pre-processing steps can be applied as a pipeline, or you might choose to ignore some of them. We will talk about tokenization, stemmers, and lemmatizers in the next section in detail. We will also talk about the variants, and when to use one case over the other.

Now that you have an idea of what text wrangling is, try to connect to any one of the databases using one of the Python modules described in the preceding image.

Text cleansing

Once we have parsed the text from a variety of data sources, the challenge is to make sense of this raw data. Text cleansing is loosely used for most of the cleaning to be done on text, depending on the data source, parsing performance, external noise and so on. In that sense, what we did in *Chapter 1, Introduction to Natural Language Processing* for cleaning the html using `html_clean`, can be labeled as text cleansing. In another case, where we are parsing a PDF, there could be unwanted noisy characters, non `ASCII` characters to be removed, and so on. Before going on to next steps we want to remove these to get a clean text to process further. With a data source like `xml`, we might only be interested in some specific elements of the tree, with databases we may have to manipulate splitters, and sometimes we are only interested in specific columns. In summary, any process that is done with the aim to make the text cleaner and to remove all the noise surrounding the text can be termed as text cleansing. There are no clear boundaries between the terms data munging, text cleansing, and data wrangling they can be used interchangeably in a similar context. In the next few sections, we will talk about some of the most common pre-processing steps while doing any NLP task.

Sentence splitter

Some of the NLP applications require splitting a large raw text into sentences to get more meaningful information out. Intuitively, a sentence is an acceptable unit of conversation. When it comes to computers, it is a harder task than it looks. A typical sentence splitter can be something as simple as splitting the string on (`.`), to something as complex as a predictive classifier to identify sentence boundaries:

```
>>>inputstring = ' This is an example sent. The sentence splitter will split on sent markers. Ohh really !!'
>>>from nltk.tokenize import sent_tokenize
>>>all_sent = sent_tokenize(inputstring)
>>>print all_sent
[' This is an example sent', 'The sentence splitter will split on markers.','Ohh really !!']
```

We are trying to split the raw text string into a list of sentences. The preceding function, `sent_tokenize`, internally uses a sentence boundary detection algorithm that comes pre-built into NLTK. If your application requires a custom sentence splitter, there are ways that we can train a sentence splitter of our own:

```
>>>import nltk.tokenize.punkt
>>>tokenizer = nltk.tokenize.punkt.PunktSentenceTokenizer()
```

The preceding sentence splitter is available in all the 17 languages. You just need to specify the respective pickle object. In my experience, this is good enough to deal with a variety of the text corpus, and there is a lesser chance that you will have to build your own.

Tokenization

A word (*Token*) is the minimal unit that a machine can understand and process. So any text string cannot be further processed without going through tokenization. Tokenization is the process of splitting the raw string into meaningful tokens. The complexity of tokenization varies according to the need of the NLP application, and the complexity of the language itself. For example, in English it can be as simple as choosing only words and numbers through a regular expression. But for Chinese and Japanese, it will be a very complex task.

```
>>>s = "Hi Everyone !    hola gr8" # simplest tokenizer
>>>print s.split()
['Hi', 'Everyone', '!', 'hola', 'gr8']
>>>from nltk.tokenize import word_tokenize
>>>word_tokenize(s)
['Hi', 'Everyone', '!', 'hola', 'gr8']
>>>from nltk.tokenize import regexp_tokenize, wordpunct_tokenize,
blankline_tokenize
>>>regexp_tokenize(s, pattern='\w+')
['Hi', 'Everyone', 'hola', 'gr8']
>>>regexp_tokenize(s, pattern='\d+')
['8']
>>>wordpunct_tokenize(s)
['Hi', ',', 'Everyone', '!!', 'hola', 'gr8']
>>>blankline_tokenize(s)
['Hi, Everyone !!  hola gr8']
```

In the preceding code we have used various tokenizers. To start with we used the simplest: the `split()` method of Python strings. This is the most basic tokenizer, that uses white space as delimiter. But the `split()` method itself can be configured for some more complex tokenization. In the preceding example, you will find hardly a difference between the `s.split()` and `word_tokenize` methods.

The `word_tokenize` method is a generic and more robust method of tokenization for any kind of text corpus. The `word_tokenize` method comes pre-built with NLTK. If you are not able to access it, you made some mistakes in installing NLTK data. Please refer to *Chapter 1, Introduction to Natural Language Processing* for installation.

There are two most commonly used tokenizers. The first is `word_tokenize`, which is the default one, and will work in most cases. The other is `regex_tokenize`, which is more of a customized tokenizer for the specific needs of the user. Most of the other tokenizers can be derived from regex tokenizers. You can also build a very specific tokenizer using a different pattern. In line 8 of the preceding code, we split the same string with the regex tokenizer. We use `\w+` as a regular expression, which means we need all the words and digits from the string, and other symbols can be used as a splitter, same as what we do in line 10 where we specify `\d+` as regex. The result will produce only digits from the string.

Can you build a regex tokenizer that will only select words that are either small, capitals, numbers, or money symbols?

Hint: Just look for the regular expression for the preceding query and use a `regex_tokenize`.

You can also have a look at some of the demos available online: `http://text-processing.com/demo`.

Stemming

Stemming, in literal terms, is the process of cutting down the branches of a tree to its stem. So effectively, with the use of some basic rules, any token can be cut down to its stem. Stemming is more of a crude rule-based process by which we want to club together different variations of the token. For example, the word *eat* will have variations like eating, eaten, eats, and so on. In some applications, as it does not make sense to differentiate between eat and eaten, we typically use stemming to club both grammatical variances to the root of the word. While stemming is used most of the time for its simplicity, there are cases of complex language or complex NLP tasks where it's necessary to use lemmatization instead. Lemmatization is a more robust and methodical way of combining grammatical variations to the root of a word.

In the following snippet, we show a few stemmers:

```
>>>from nltk.stem import PorterStemmer # import Porter stemmer
>>>from nltk.stem.lancaster import LancasterStemmer
>>>from nltk.stem.Snowball import SnowballStemmer
>>>pst = PorterStemmer()   # create obj of the PorterStemmer
>>>lst = LancasterStemmer() # create obj of LancasterStemmer
>>>lst.stem("eating")
eat
>>>pst.stem("shopping")
shop
```

A basic rule-based stemmer, like removing *-s/es* or *-ing* or *-ed* can give you a precision of more than 70 percent, while **Porter stemmer** also uses more rules and can achieve very good accuracies.

We are creating different stemmer objects, and applying a `stem()` method on the string. As you can see, there is not much of a difference when you look at a simple example, however there are many stemming algorithms around, and the precision and performance of them differ. You may want to have a look at `http://www.nltk.org/api/nltk.stem.html` for more details. I have used Porter Stemmer most often, and if you are working with English, it's good enough. There is a family of **Snowball stemmers** that can be used for Dutch, English, French, German, Italian, Portuguese, Romanian, Russian, and so on. I also came across a light weight stemmer for Hindi on `http://research.variancia.com/hindi_stemmer`.

I would suggest a study of all the stemmers for those who want to explore more about stemmers on `http://en.wikipedia.org/wiki/Stemming`.

But most users can live with Porter and Snowball stemmer for a large number of use cases. In modern NLP applications, sometimes people even ignore stemming as a pre-processing step, so it typically depends on your domain and application. I would also like to tell you the fact that if you want to use some NLP taggers, like Part of Speech tagger (POS), NER or dependency parser, you should avoid stemming, because stemming will modify the token and this can result in a different result. We will go into this further when we talk about taggers in general.

Lemmatization

Lemmatization is a more methodical way of converting all the grammatical/inflected forms of the root of the word. Lemmatization uses context and part of speech to determine the inflected form of the word and applies different normalization rules for each part of speech to get the root word (*lemma*):

```
>>>from nltk.stem import WordNetLemmatizer
>>>wlem = WordNetLemmatizer()
>>>wlem.lemmatize("ate")
eat
```

Here, `WordNetLemmatizer` is using `wordnet`, which takes a word and searches `wordnet`, a semantic dictionary. It also uses a morph analysis to cut to the root and search for the specific lemma (variation of the word). Hence, in our example it is possible to get *eat* for the given variation *ate*, which was never possible with stemming.

- Can you explain what the difference is between Stemming and lemmatization?
- Can you come up with a Porter stemmer (Rule-based) for your native language?
- Why would it be harder to implement a stemmer for languages like Chinese?

Stop word removal

Stop word removal is one of the most commonly used preprocessing steps across different NLP applications. The idea is simply removing the words that occur commonly across all the documents in the corpus. Typically, articles and pronouns are generally classified as stop words. These words have no significance in some of the NLP tasks like information retrieval and classification, which means these words are not very discriminative. On the contrary, in some NLP applications stop word removal will have very little impact. Most of the time, the stop word list for the given language is a well hand-curated list of words that occur most commonly across corpuses. While the stop word lists for most languages are available online, these are also ways to automatically generate the stop word list for the given corpus. A very simple way to build a stop word list is based on word's document frequency (Number of documents the word presents), where the words present across the corpus can be treated as stop words. Enough research has been done to get the optimum list of stop words for some specific corpus. NLTK comes with a pre-built list of stop words for around 22 languages.

To implement the process of stop word removal, below is code that uses NLTK stop word. You can also create a dictionary on a lookup based approach like we did in *Chapter 1, Introduction to Natural Language Processing*.

```
>>>from nltk.corpus import stopwords
>>>stoplist = stopwords.words('english') # config the language name
# NLTK supports 22 languages for removing the stop words
>>>text = "This is just a test"
>>>cleanwordlist = [word for word in text.split() if word not in
stoplist]
# apart from just and test others are stopwords
['test']
```

In the preceding code snippet, we have deployed a cleaner version of the same stop word removal we did in *Chapter 1, Introduction to Natural Language Processing*. Previously, we were using a lookup based approach. Even in this case, NLTK internally did a very similar approach. I would recommend using the NLTK list of stop words, because this is more of a standardized list, and this is robust when compared to any other implementation. We also have a way to use similar methods for other languages by just passing the language name as a parameter to the stop words constructor.

- What's the math behind removing stop words?
- Can we perform other NLP operations after stop word removal?

Rare word removal

This is very intuitive, as some of the words that are very unique in nature like names, brands, product names, and some of the noise characters, such as html leftouts, also need to be removed for different NLP tasks. For example, it would be really bad to use names as a predictor for a text classification problem, even if they come out as a significant predictor. We will talk about this further in subsequent chapters. We definitely don't want all these noisy tokens to be present. We also use length of the words as a criteria for removing words with very a short length or a very long length:

```
>>># tokens is a list of all tokens in corpus
>>>freq_dist = nltk.FreqDist(token)
>>>rarewords = freq_dist.keys()[-50:]
>>>after_rare_words = [ word for word in token not in rarewords]
```

We are using the `FreqDist()` function to get the distribution of the terms in the corpus, selecting the rarest one into a list, and then filtering our original corpus. We can also do it for individual documents, as well.

Spell correction

It is not a necessary to use a spellchecker for all NLP applications, but some use cases require you to use a basic spellcheck. We can create a very basic spellchecker by just using a dictionary lookup. There are some enhanced string algorithms that have been developed for fuzzy string matching. One of the most commonly used is `edit-distance`. NLTK also provides you with a variety of metrics module that has `edit_distance`.

```
>>>from nltk.metrics import edit_distance
>>>edit_distance("rain","shine")
3
```

We will cover this module in more detail in advanced chapters. We also have one of the most elegant codes for spellchecker from Peter Norvig, which is quite easy to understand and written in pure Python.

I would recommend that anyone who works with natural language processing visit the following link for spellcheck: `http://norvig.com/spell-correct.html`

Your turn

Here are the answers to the open-ended questions:

- Try to connect any of the data base using pyodbc.

  `https://code.google.com/p/pyodbc/wiki/GettingStarted`

- Can you build a regex tokenizer that will only select words that are either small, capitals, numbers or money symbols?

  [\w+] selects all the words and numbers [a-z A-Z 0-9] and [\$] will match money symbol.

- What's the difference between Stemming and lemmatization?

  Stemming is more of a rule-based approach to get the root of the word's grammatical forms, while lemmatization also considers context and the POS of the given word, then applies rules specific to grammatical variants. Stemmers are easier to implement and the processing time is faster than lemmatizer.

- Can you come up with a Porter stemmer (Rule-based) for your native language?

  Hint: `http://tartarus.org/martin/PorterStemmer/Python.txt`

  `http://Snowball.tartarus.org/algorithms/english/stemmer.html`

- Can we perform other NLP operations after stop word removal?

  No; never. All the typical NLP applications like POS tagging, chunking, and so on will need context to generate the tags for the given text. Once we remove the stop word, we lose the context.

- Why would it be harder to implement a stemmer for languages like Hindi or Chinese?

  Indian languages are morphologically rich and it's hard to token the Chinese; there are challenges with the normalization of the symbols, so it's even harder to implement steamer. We will talk about these challenges in advanced chapters.

Summary

In this chapter we talked about all the data wrangling/munging in the context of text. We went through some of the most common data sources, and how to parse them with Python packages. We talked about tokenization in depth, from a very basic string method to a custom regular expression based tokenizer.

We talked about stemming and lemmatization, and the various types of stemmers that can be used, as well as the pros and cons of each of them. We also discussed the stop word removal process, why it's important, when to remove stop words, and when it's not needed. We also briefly touched upon removing rare words and why it's important in text cleansing—both stop word and rare word removal are essentially removing outliers from the frequency distribution. We also referred to spell correction. There is no limit to what you can do with text wrangling and text cleansing. Every text corpus has new challenges, and a new kind of noise that needs to be removed. You will get to learn over time what kind of pre-processing works best for your corpus, and what can be ignored.

In the next chapter will see some of the NLP related pre-processing, like POS tagging, chunking, and NER. I am leaving answers or hints for some of the open questions that we asked in the chapter.

3
Part of Speech Tagging

In previous chapters, we talked about all the preprocessing steps we need, in order to work with any text corpus. You should now be comfortable about parsing any kind of text and should be able to clean it. You should be able to perform all text preprocessing, such as Tokenization, Stemming, and Stop Word removal on any text. You can perform and customize all the preprocessing tools to fit your needs. So far, we have mainly discussed generic preprocessing to be done with text documents. Now let's move on to more intense NLP preprocessing steps.

In this chapter, we will discuss what part of speech tagging is, and what the significance of POS is in the context of NLP applications. We will also learn how to use NLTK to extract meaningful information using tagging and various taggers used for NLP intense applications. Lastly, we will learn how NLTK can be used to tag a named entity. We will discuss in detail the various NLP taggers and also give a small snippet to help you get going. We will also see the best practices, and where to use what kind of tagger. By the end of this chapter, readers will learn:

- What is Part of speech tagging and how important it is in context of NLP
- What are the different ways of doing POS tagging using NLTK
- How to build a custom POS tagger using NLTK

What is Part of speech tagging

In your childhood, you may have heard the term **Part of Speech** (**POS**). It can really take good amount of time to get the hang of what adjectives and adverbs actually are. What exactly is the difference? Think about building a system where we can encode all this knowledge. It may look very easy, but for many decades, coding this knowledge into a machine learning model was a very hard NLP problem. I think current state of the art POS tagging algorithms can predict the POS of the given word with a higher degree of precision (that is approximately 97 percent). But still lots of research going on in the area of POS tagging.

Languages like English have many tagged corpuses available in the news and other domains. This has resulted in many state of the art algorithms. Some of these taggers are generic enough to be used across different domains and varieties of text. But in specific use cases, the POS might not perform as expected. For these use cases, we might need to build a POS tagger from scratch. To understand the internals of a POS, we need to have a basic understanding of some of the machine learning techniques. We will talk about some of these in *Chapter 6, Text Classification*, but we have to discuss the basics in order to build a custom POS tagger to fit our needs.

First, we will learn some of the pertained POS taggers available, along with a set of tokens. You can get the POS of individual words as a **tuple**. We will then move on to the internal workings of some of these taggers, and we will also talk about building a custom tagger from scratch.

When we talk about POS, the most frequent POS notification used is Penn Treebank:

Tag	Description
NNP	Proper noun, singular
NNPS	Proper noun, plural
PDT	Pre determiner
POS	Possessive ending
PRP	Personal pronoun
PRP$	Possessive pronoun
RB	Adverb
RBR	Adverb, comparative
RBS	Adverb, superlative
RP	Particle
SYM	Symbol (mathematical or scientific)
TO	to
UH	Interjection
VB	Verb, base form
VBD	Verb, past tense

Tag	Description
VBG	Verb, gerund/present participle
VBN	Verb, past
WP	Wh-pronoun
WP$	Possessive wh-pronoun
WRB	Wh-adverb
#	Pound sign
$	Dollar sign
.	Sentence-final punctuation
,	Comma
:	Colon, semi-colon
(	Left bracket character
)	Right bracket character
"	Straight double quote
'	Left open single quote
"	Left open double quote
'	Right close single quote
"	Right open double quote

Looks pretty much like what we learned in primary school English class, right? Now once we have an understanding about what these tags mean, we can run an experiment:

```
>>>import nltk
>>>from nltk import word_tokenize
>>>s = "I was watching TV"
>>>print nltk.pos_tag(word_tokenize(s))
[('I', 'PRP'), ('was', 'VBD'), ('watching', 'VBG'), ('TV', 'NN')]
```

If you just want to use POS for a corpus like news or something similar, you just need to know the preceding three lines of code. In this code, we are tokenizing a piece of text and using NLTK's `pos_tag` method to get a tuple of (word, `pos-tag`). This is one of the pre-trained POS taggers that comes with NLTK.

> It's internally using the `maxent` classifier (will discuss these classifiers in advanced chapters) trained model to predict to which class of tag a particular word belongs.
>
> To get more details you can use the following link:
>
> `https://github.com/nltk/nltk/blob/develop/nltk/tag/__init__.py`

NLTK has used python's powerful data structures efficiently, so we have a lot more flexibility in terms of use of the results of NLTK outputs.

You must be wondering what could be a typical use of POS in a real application. In a typical preprocessing, we might want to look for all the nouns. Now this code snippet will give us all the nouns in the given sentence:

```
>>>tagged = nltk.pos_tag(word_tokenize(s))
>>>allnoun = [word for word,pos in tagged if pos in ['NN','NNP'] ]
```

Try to answer the following questions:

- Can we remove stop words before POS tagging?
- How can we get all the verbs in the sentence?

Stanford tagger

Another awesome feature of NLTK is that it also has many wrappers around other pre-trained taggers, such as **Stanford tools**. A common example of a POS tagger is shown here:

```
>>>from nltk.tag.stanford import POSTagger
>>>import nltk
>>>stan_tagger = POSTagger('models/english-bidirectional-distdim.
tagger','standford-postagger.jar')
>>>tokens = nltk.word_tokenize(s)
>>>stan_tagger.tag(tokens)
```

To use the above code, you need to download the Stanford tagger from `http://nlp.stanford.edu/software/stanford-postagger-full-2014-08-27.zip`. Extract both the jar and model into a folder, and give an absolute path in argument for the `POSTagger`.

Summarizing this, there are mainly two ways to achieve any tagging task in NLTK:

1. Using NLTK's or another lib's pre-trained tagger, and applying it on the test data. Both preceding taggers should be sufficient to deal with any POS tagging task that deals with plain English text, and the corpus is not very domain specific.
2. Building or Training a tagger to be used on test data. This is to deal with a very specific use case and to develop a customized tagger.

Let's dig deeper into what goes on inside a typical POS tagger.

Diving deep into a tagger

A typical tagger uses a lot of trained data, with sentences tagged for each word that will be the POS tag attached to it. Tagging is purely manual and looks like this:

```
Well/UH what/WP do/VBP you/PRP think/VB about/IN the/DT idea/NN of/IN ,/,
uh/UH ,/, kids/NNS having/VBG to/TO do/VB public/JJ service/NN work/NN
for/IN a/DT year/NN ?/.Do/VBP you/PRP think/VBP it/PRP 's/BES a/DT ,/,
```

The preceding sample is taken from the Penn Treebank switchboard corpus. People have done lot of manual work tagging large corpuses. There is a **Linguistic Data Consortium (LDC)** where people have dedicated so much time to tagging for different languages, different kinds of text and different kinds of tagging like POS, dependency parsing, and discourse (will talk about these later).

You can get all these resources and more information about them at `https://www.ldc.upenn.edu/`. (**LDC** provides a fraction of data for free but you can also purchase the entire tagged corpus. NLTK has approximately 10 percent of the PTB.)

If we also want to train our own POS tagger, we have to do the tagging exercise for our specific domain. This kind of tagging will require domain experts.

Typically, tagging problems like POS tagging are seen as sequence labeling problems or a classification problem where people have tried generative and discriminative models to predict the right tag for the given token.

Instead of jumping directly in to more sophisticated examples, let's start with some simple approaches for tagging.

The following snippet gives us the frequency distribution of POS tags in the Brown corpus:

```
>>>from nltk.corpus import brown
>>>import nltk
>>>tags = [tag for (word, tag) in brown.tagged_words(categories='news')]
>>>print nltk.FreqDist(tags)
<FreqDist: 'NN': 13162, 'IN': 10616, 'AT': 8893, 'NP': 6866, ',': 5133,
'NNS': 5066, '.': 4452, 'JJ': 4392 >
```

We can see `NN` comes as the most frequent tag, so let's start building a very naïve POS tagger, by assigning `NN` as a tag to all the test words. NLTK has a `DefaultTagger` function that can be used for this. `DefaultTagger` function is part of the Sequence tagger, which will be discussed next. There is a function called `evaluate()` that gives the accuracy of the correctly predicted POS of the words. This is used to benchmark the tagger against the brown corpus. In the `default_tagger` case, we are getting approximately 13 percent of the predictions correct. We will use the same benchmark for all the taggers moving forward.

```
>>>brown_tagged_sents = brown.tagged_sents(categories='news')
>>>default_tagger = nltk.DefaultTagger('NN')
>>>print default_tagger.evaluate(brown_tagged_sents)
0.130894842572
```

Sequential tagger

Not surprisingly, the above tagger performed poorly. The `DefaultTagger` is part of a base class `SequentialBackoffTagger` that serves tags based on the Sequence. Tagger tries to model the tags based on the context, and if it is not able to predict the tag correctly, it consults a `BackoffTagger`. Typically, the `DefaultTagger` parameter could be used as a `BackoffTagger`.

Let's move on to more sophisticated sequential taggers.

N-gram tagger

N-gram tagger is a subclass of `SequentialTagger`, where the tagger takes previous *n* words in the context, to predict the POS tag for the given token. There are variations of these taggers where people have tried it with `UnigramsTagger`, `BigramsTagger`, and `TrigramTagger`:

```
>>>from nltk.tag import UnigramTagger
>>>from nltk.tag import DefaultTagger
>>>from nltk.tag import BigramTagger
>>>from nltk.tag import TrigramTagger
# we are dividing the data into a test and train to evaluate our taggers.
>>>train_data = brown_tagged_sents[:int(len(brown_tagged_sents) * 0.9)]
>>>test_data = brown_tagged_sents[int(len(brown_tagged_sents) * 0.9):]
>>>unigram_tagger = UnigramTagger(train_data,backoff=default_tagger)
>>>print unigram_tagger.evaluate(test_data)
0.826195866853
>>>bigram_tagger = BigramTagger(train_data, backoff=unigram_tagger)
>>>print bigram_tagger.evaluate(test_data)
0.835300351655
>>>trigram_tagger = TrigramTagger(train_data,backoff=bigram_tagger)
>>>print trigram_tagger.evaluate(test_data)
0.83327713281
```

Unigram just considers the conditional frequency of tags and predicts the most frequent tag for the every given token. The `bigram_tagger` parameter will consider the tags of the given word and the previous word, and tag as tuple to get the given tag for the test word. The `TrigramTagger` parameter looks for the previous two words with a similar process.

It's very evident that coverage of the `TrigramTagger` parameter will be less and the accuracy of that instance will be high. On the other hand, `UnigramTagger` will have better coverage. To deal with this tradeoff between precision/recall, we combine the three taggers in the preceding snippet. First it will look for the trigram of the given word sequence for predicting the tag; if not found it `Backoff` to `BigramTagger` parameter and to a `UnigramTagger` parameter and in end to a `NN` tag.

Regex tagger

There is one more class of sequential tagger that is a regular expression based taggers. Here, instead of looking for the exact word, we can define a regular expression, and at the same time we can define the corresponding tag for the given expressions. For example, in the following code we have provided some of the most common regex patterns to get the different parts of speech. We know some of the patterns related to each POS category, for example we know the articles in English and we know that anything that ends with *ness* will be an adjective. Instead, we will write a bunch of regex and a pure python code, and the NLTK `RegexpTagger` parameter will provide an elegant way of building a pattern based POS. This can also be used to induce domain related POS patterns.

```
>>>from nltk.tag.sequential import RegexpTagger
>>>regexp_tagger = RegexpTagger(
         [( r'^-?[0-9]+(.[0-9]+)?$', 'CD'),    # cardinal numbers
          ( r'(The|the|A|a|An|an)$', 'AT'),    # articles
          ( r'.*able$', 'JJ'),                 # adjectives
          ( r'.*ness$', 'NN'),             # nouns formed from adj
          ( r'.*ly$', 'RB'),               # adverbs
          ( r'.*s$', 'NNS'),               # plural nouns
          ( r'.*ing$', 'VBG'),             # gerunds
          (r'.*ed$', 'VBD'),               # past tense verbs
          (r'.*', 'NN')                    # nouns (default)
          ])
>>>print regexp_tagger.evaluate(test_data)
0.303627342358
```

We can see that by just using some of the obvious patterns for POS we are able to reach approximately 30 percent in terms of accuracy. If we combine regex taggers, such as the `BackoffTagger`, we might improve the performance. The other use case for regex tagger is in the preprocessing step, where instead of using a raw Python function `string.sub()`, we can use this tagger to tag date patterns, money patterns, location patterns and so on.

- Can you modify the code of a hybrid tagger in the N-gram tagger section to work with Regex tagger? Does that improve performance?
- Can you write a tagger that tags Date and Money expressions?

Brill tagger

Brill tagger is a transformation based tagger, where the idea is to start with a guess for the given tag and, in next iteration, go back and fix the errors based on the next set of rules the tagger learned. It's also a supervised way of tagging, but unlike N-gram tagging where we count the N-gram patterns in training data, we look for transformation rules.

If the tagger starts with a `Unigram` / `Bigram` tagger with an acceptable accuracy, then brill tagger, instead looking for a trigram tuple, will be looking for rules based on tags, position and the word itself.

An example rule could be:

Replace `NN` with `VB` when the previous word is `TO`.

After we already have some tags based on `UnigramTagger`, we can refine if with just one simple rule. This is an interactive process. With a few iterations and some more optimized rules, the brill tagger can outperform some of the N-gram taggers. The only piece of advice is to look out for over-fitting of the tagger for the training set.

You can also look at the work here for more example rules.

`http://stp.lingfil.uu.se/~bea/publ/megyesi-BrillsPoSTagger.pdf`

- Can you try to write more rules based on your observation?
- Try to combine brill tagger with `UnigramTagger`.

Machine learning based tagger

Until now we have just used some of the pre-trained taggers from NLTK or Stanford. While we have used them in the examples in previous section, the internals of the taggers are still a black box to us. For example, `pos_tag` internally uses a **Maximum Entropy Classifier** (**MEC**). While `StanfordTagger` also uses a modified version of Maximum Entropy. These are discriminatory models. While there are many **Hidden Markov Model** (**HMM**) and **Conditional Random Field** (**CRF**) based taggers, these are generative models.

Covering all of these topics is beyond the scope of the book. I would highly recommend the NLP class for a great understanding of these concepts. We will cover some of the classification techniques in *Chapter 6, Text Classification*, but some of these are very advanced topics in NLP, and will need more attention.

If I have to explain in short, the way to categorize POS tagging problem is either as a classification problem where given a word and the features like previous word, context, morphological variation, and so on. We classify the given word into a POS category, while the others try to model it as a generative model using the similar features. It's for the reader's reference to go over some of these topics using links in the tips.

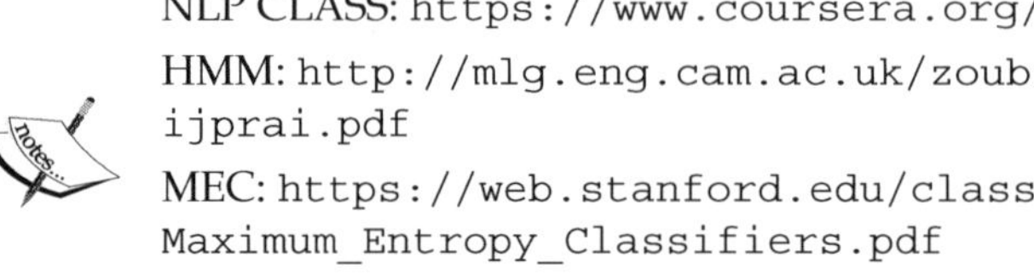

NLP CLASS: `https://www.coursera.org/course/nlp`

HMM: `http://mlg.eng.cam.ac.uk/zoubin/papers/ijprai.pdf`

MEC: `https://web.stanford.edu/class/cs124/lec/Maximum_Entropy_Classifiers.pdf`

`http://nlp.stanford.edu/software/tagger.shtml`

Named Entity Recognition (NER)

Aside from POS, one of the most common labeling problems is finding entities in the text. Typically NER constitutes name, location, and organizations. There are NER systems that tag more entities than just three of these. The problem can be seen as a sequence, labeling the Named entities using the context and other features. There is a lot more research going on in this area of NLP where people are trying to tag Biomedical entities, product entities in retail, and so on. Again, there are two ways of tagging the NER using NLTK. One is by using the pre-trained NER model that just scores the test data, the other is to build a Machine learning based model. NLTK provides the `ne_chunk()` method and a wrapper around Stanford NER tagger for Named Entity Recognition.

NER tagger

NLTK provides a method for Named Entity Extraction: `ne_chunk`. We have shown a small snippet to demonstrate how to use it for tagging any sentence. This method will require you to preprocess the text to tokenize for sentences, tokens, and POS tags in the same order to be able to tag for Named entities. NLTK used `ne_chunking`, where chunking is nothing but tagging multiple tokens to a call it a meaningful entity.

NE chunking is loosely used in the same way as Named entity:

```
>>>import nltk
>>>from nltk import ne_chunk
>>>Sent = "Mark is studying at Stanford University in California"
>>>print(ne_chunk(nltk.pos_tag(word_tokenize(sent)), binary=False))
(S
  (PERSON Mark/NNP)
  is/VBZ
  studying/VBG
  at/IN
  (ORGANIZATION Stanford/NNP University/NNP)
  in/IN
  NY(GPE California/NNP)))
```

The `ne_chunking` method recognizes people (names), places (location), and organizations. If binary is set to `True` then it provides the output for the entire sentence tree and tags everything. Setting it to `False` will give us detailed person, location and organizations information, as with the preceding example using the Stanford NER Tagger.

Similar to the POS tagger, NLTK also has a wrapper around Stanford NER. This NER tagger has better accuracy. The code following snippet will let you use the tagger. You can see in the given example that we are able to tag all the entities with just three lines of code:

```
>>>from nltk.tag.stanford import NERTagger
>>>st = NERTagger('<PATH>/stanford-ner/classifiers/all.3class.distsim.
crf.ser.gz',...                '<PATH>/stanford-ner/stanford-ner.jar')
>>>st.tag('Rami Eid is studying at Stony Brook University in NY'.split())
[('Rami', 'PERSON'), ('Eid', 'PERSON'), ('is', 'O'), ('studying', 'O'),
('at', 'O'), ('Stony', 'ORGANIZATION'), ('Brook', 'ORGANIZATION'),
('University', 'ORGANIZATION'), ('in', 'O'), ('NY', 'LOCATION')]
```

If you observe closely, even with a very small test sentence, we can say Stanford Tagger outperformed the NLTK `ne_chunk` tagger.

Now, these kinds of NER taggers are a nice solution for a generic kind of entity tagging, but we have to train our own tagger, when it comes, to tag domain specific entities like biomedical and product names, so we have to build our own NER system. I would also recommend an NER Calais. It has ways of tagging not just typical NER, but also some more entities. The performance of this tagger is also very good:

`https://code.google.com/p/python-calais/`

Your Turn

Here are the answers to the questions posed in the above sections:

- Can we remove stop words before POS tagging?

  No; If we remove the stop words, we will lose the context, and some of the POS taggers (Pre-Trained model) use word context as features to give the POS of the given word.

- How can we get all the verbs in the sentence?

  We can get all the verbs in the sentence by using `pos_tag`

```
>>>tagged = nltk.pos_tag(word_tokenize(s))
>>>allverbs = [word for word,pos in tagged if pos in ['VB','VBD','VBG'] ]
```

- Can you modify the code of the hybrid tagger in the N-gram tagger section to work with Regex tagger? Does that improve performance?

  Yes. We can modify the code of the hybrid tagger in the N-gram tagger section to work with the Regex tagger:

```
>>>print unigram_tagger.evaluate(test_data,backoff= regexp_tagger)
>>>bigram_tagger = BigramTagger(train_data, backoff=unigram_tagger)
>>>print bigram_tagger.evaluate(test_data)
>>>trigram_tagger=TrigramTagger(train_data,backoff=bigram_tagger)
>>>print trigram_tagger.evaluate(test_data)
0.857122212053
0.866708415627
0.863914446746
```

  The performance improves as we add some basic pattern-based rules, instead of predicting the most frequent tag.

- Can you write a tagger that tags Date and Money expressions?

  Yes, we can write a tagger that tags Date and Money expressions. Following is the code:

```
>>>date_regex = RegexpTagger([(r'(\d{2})[/.-](\d{2})[/.-](\d{4})$','DATE'),(r'\$','MONEY')])
>>>test_tokens = "I will be flying on sat 10-02-2014 with around 10M $ ".split()
>>>print date_regex.tag(test_tokens)
```

The last two questions haven't been answered.

There can be many rules according to the reader's observation, so there is no Right / Wrong answer here.

Can you try a similar word cloud to what we did in *Chapter 1, Introduction to Natural Language Processing* with only nouns and verbs now?

References:

`https://github.com/japerk/nltk-trainer`

`http://en.wikipedia.org/wiki/Part-of-speech_tagging`

`http://en.wikipedia.org/wiki/Named-entity_recognition`

`http://www.inf.ed.ac.uk/teaching/courses/icl/nltk/tagging.pdf`

`http://www.nltk.org/api/nltk.tag.html`

Summary

This chapter was intended to expose the reader to some of the most useful NLP pre-processing steps of tagging. We have talked about the Part of Speech problem in general, including the significance of POS in the context of NLP. We also discussed the different ways we can use a pre-trained POS tagger in NLTK, how simple it is to use, and how to create wonderful applications. We then talked about all the available POS tagging options, like N-gram tagging, Regex based tagging, etc. We have developed a mix of these taggers that can be built for domain specific corpuses. We briefly talked about how a typical pre-trained tagger is built. We discussed the possible approaches to address tagging problems. We also talked about NER taggers, and how it works with NLTK. I think if, by the end of this chapter, the user understands the importance of POS and NER in general in the context of NLP, as well as how to run the snippet of codes using NLTK, I will consider this chapter successful. But the journey does not end here. We know some of the shallow NLP preprocessing steps now, and in most of the practical application POS, the NER predominantly used. In more complex NLP applications such as the Q/A system, Summarization, and Speech we need deeper NLP techniques like Chunking, Parsing, Semantics. We will talk about these in the next chapter.

4
Parsing Structure in Text

This chapter involves a better understanding of deep structure in text and also how to deep parse text and use it in various NLP applications. Now, we are equipped with various NLP preprocessing steps. Let's move to some deeper aspect of the text. The structure of language is so complex that we can describe it by various layers of structural processing. In this chapter we will touch upon all these structures in text, differentiate between them, and provide you with enough details about the usage of one of these. We will talk about **context-free grammar** (**CFG**) and how it can be implemented with NLTK. We will also look at the various parsers and how we can use some of the existing parsing methods in NLTK. We will write a shallow parser in NLTK and will again talk about NER in the context of chunking. We will also provide details about some options that exist in NLTK to do deep structural analysis. We will also try to give you some real-world use cases of information extraction and how it can be achieved by using some of the topics that you will learn in this chapter. We want you to have an understanding of these topics by the end of this chapter.

In this chapter:

- We will also see what parsing is and what is the relevance of parsing in NLP.
- We will then explore different parsers and see how we can use NLTK for parsing.
- Finally, we will see how parsing can be used for information extraction.

Shallow versus deep parsing

In deep or full parsing, typically, grammar concepts such as CFG, and **probabilistic context-free grammar (PCFG)**, and a search strategy is used to give a complete syntactic structure to a sentence. Shallow parsing is the task of parsing a limited part of the syntactic information from the given text. While deep parsing is required for more complex NLP applications, such as dialogue systems and summarization, shallow parsing is more suited for information extraction and text mining varieties of applications. I will talk about these in the next few sections with more details about their pros and cons and how we can use them for our NLP application.

The two approaches in parsing

There are mainly two views/approaches used to deal with parsing, which are as follows:

The rule-based approach	The probabilistic approach
This approach is based on rules/grammar	In this approach, you learn rules/grammar by using probabilistic models
Manual grammatical rules are coded down in CFG, and so on, in this approach	This uses observed probabilities of linguistic features
This has a top-down approach	This has a bottom-up approach
This approach includes CFG and Regex-based parser	This approach includes PCFG and the Stanford parser

Why we need parsing

I again want to take you guys back to school, where we learned grammar. Now tell me why you learnt grammar Do you really need to learn grammar? The answer is definitely yes! When we grow, we learn our native languages. Now, when we typically learn languages, we learn a small set of vocabulary. We learn to combine small chunks of phrases and then small sentences. By learning each example sentence, we learn the structure of the language. Your mom might have corrected you many times when you uttered an incorrect sentence. We apply a similar process when we try to understand the sentence, but the process is so common that we never actually pay attention to it or think about it in detail. Maybe the next time you correct someone's grammar, you will understand.

When it comes to writing a parser, we try to replicate the same process here. If we come up with a set of rules that can be used as a template to write the sentences in a proper order. We also need the words that can fit into these categories. We already talked about this process. Remember POS tagging, where we knew the category of the given word?

Now, if you've understood this, you have learned the rules of the game and what moves are valid and can be taken for a specific step. We essentially follow a very natural phenomenon of the human brain and try to emulate it. One of the simplest grammar concepts to start with is CFG, where we just need a set of rules and a set of terminal tokens.

Let's write our first grammar with very limited vocabulary and very generic rules:

```
# toy CFG
>>>from nltk import CFG
>>>toy_grammar =
nltk.CFG.fromstring(
"""
  S -> NP VP                # S indicate the entire sentence
  VP -> V NP                # VP is verb phrase the
  V -> "eats" | "drinks"    # V is verb
  NP -> Det N   # NP is noun phrase (chunk that has noun in it)
  Det -> "a" | "an" | "the" # Det is determiner used in the sentences
  N -> "president" |"Obama" |"apple"| "coke"  # N some example nouns
    """)
>>>toy_grammar.productions()
```

Now, this grammar concept can generate a finite amount of sentences. Think of a situation where you just know how to combine a noun with a verb and the only verbs and nouns you knew were the ones we used in the preceding code. Some of the example sentences we can form from these are:

- President eats apple
- Obama drinks coke

Now, understand what's happening here. Our mind has created a grammar concept to parse based on the preceding rules and substitutes whatever vocabulary we have. If we are able to parse correctly, we understand the meaning.

So, effectively, the grammar we learnt at school constituted the useful rules of English. We still use those and also keep enhancing them and these are the same rules we use to understand all English sentences. However, today's rules do not apply to William Shakespeare's body of work.

On the other hand, the same grammar can construct meaningless sentences such as:

- Apple eats coke
- President drinks Obama

When it comes to a **syntactic parser**, there is a chance that a syntactically formed sentence could be meaningless. To get to the semantics, we need a deeper understanding of semantics structure of the sentence. I encourage you to look for a semantic parser in case you are interested in these aspects of language.

Different types of parsers

A parser processes an input string by using a set of grammatical rules and builds one or more rules that construct a grammar concept. Grammar is a declarative specification of a well-formed sentence. A parser is a procedural interpretation of grammar. It searches through the space of a variety of trees and finds an optimal tree for the given sentence. We will go through some of the parsers available and briefly touch upon their workings in detail for awareness, as well as for practical purposes.

A recursive descent parser

One of the most straightforward forms of parsing is recursive descent parsing. This is a top-down process in which the parser attempts to verify that the syntax of the input stream is correct, as it is read from left to right. A basic operation necessary for this involves reading characters from the input stream and matching them with the terminals from the grammar that describes the syntax of the input. Our recursive descent parser will look ahead one character and advance the input stream reading pointer when it gets a proper match.

A shift-reduce parser

The shift-reduce parser is a simple kind of bottom-up parser. As is common with all bottom-up parsers, a shift-reduce parser tries to find a sequence of words and phrases that correspond to the right-hand side of a grammar production and replaces them with the left-hand side of the production, until the whole sentence is reduced.

A chart parser

We will apply the algorithm design technique of dynamic programming to the parsing problem. Dynamic programming stores intermediate results and reuses them when appropriate, achieving significant efficiency gains. This technique can be applied to syntactic parsing. This allows us to store partial solutions to the parsing task and then allows us to look them up when necessary in order to efficiently arrive at a complete solution. This approach to parsing is known as chart parsing.

For a better understanding of the parsers, you can go through an example at `http://www.nltk.org/howto/parse.html`.

A regex parser

A regex parser uses a regular expression defined in the form of grammar on top of a POS-tagged string. The parser will use these regular expressions to parse the given sentences and generate a parse tree out of this. A working example of the regex parser is given here:

```
# Regex parser
>>>chunk_rules=ChunkRule("<.*>+","chunk everything")
>>>import nltk
>>>from nltk.chunk.regexp import *
>>>reg_parser = RegexpParser('''
        NP: {<DT>? <JJ>* <NN>*}       # NP
         P: {<IN>}                    # Preposition
         V: {<V.*>}                   # Verb
        PP: {<P> <NP>}                # PP -> P NP
        VP: {<V> <NP|PP>*}            # VP -> V (NP|PP)*
  ''')
>>>test_sent="Mr. Obama played a big role in the Health insurance bill"
>>>test_sent_pos=nltk.pos_tag(nltk.word_tokenize(test_sent))
>>>paresed_out=reg_parser.parse(test_sent_pos)
>>> print paresed_out
Tree('S', [('Mr.', 'NNP'), ('Obama', 'NNP'), Tree('VP', [Tree('V',
[('played', 'VBD')]), Tree('NP', [('a', 'DT'), ('big', 'JJ'), ('role',
'NN')])]), Tree('P', [('in', 'IN')]), ('Health', 'NNP'), Tree('NP',
[('insurance', 'NN'), ('bill', 'NN')])])
```

The following is a graphical representation of the tree for the preceding code:

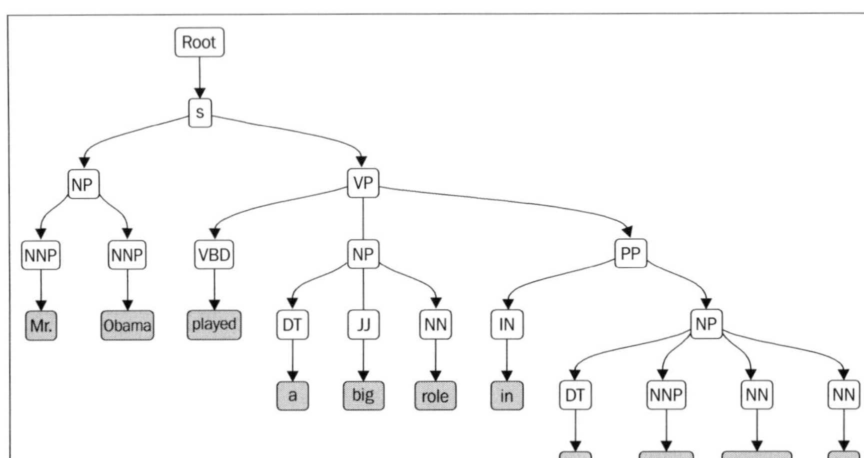

In the current example, we define the kind of patterns (a regular expression of the POS) we think will make a phrase, for example, anything that `{<DT>? <JJ>* <NN>*}` has a starting determiner followed by an adjective and then a noun is mostly a noun phrase. Now, this is more of a linguistic rule that we have defined to get the rule-based parse tree.

Dependency parsing

Dependency parsing (DP) is a modern parsing mechanism. The main concept of DP is that each linguistic unit (*words*) is connected with each other by a directed link. These links are called **dependencies** in linguistics. There is a lot of work going on in the current parsing community. While **phrase structure parsing** is still widely used for free word order languages (Czech and Turkish), dependency parsing has turned out to be more efficient.

A very clear distinction can be made by looking at the parse tree generated by phrase structure grammar and dependency grammar for a given example, as the sentence "The big dog chased the cat". The parse tree for the preceding sentence is:

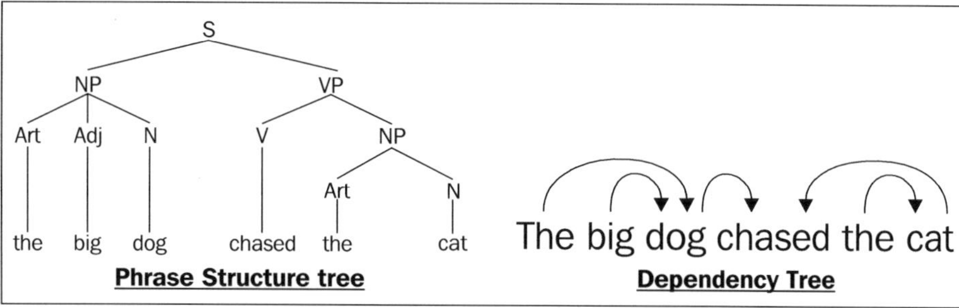

If we look at both parse trees, the phrase structures try to capture the relationship between words and phrases and then eventually between phrases. While a dependency tree just looks for a dependency between words, for example, *big* is totally dependent on *dog*.

NLTK provides a couple of ways to do dependency parsing. One of them is to use a **probabilistic**, **projective dependency parser**, but it has the restriction of training with a limited set of training data. One of the state of the art dependency parsers is a Stanford parser. Fortunately, NLTK has a wrapper around it and in the following example, I will talk about how to use a Stanford parser with NLTK:

```
# Stanford Parser [Very useful]
>>>from nltk.parse.stanford import StanfordParser
>>>english_parser = StanfordParser('stanford-parser.jar', 'stanford-
parser-3.4-models.jar')
>>>english_parser.raw_parse_sents(("this is the english parser test")
Parse
(ROOT
  (S
    (NP (DT this))
    (VP (VBZ is)
      (NP (DT the) (JJ english) (NN parser) (NN test)))))
Universal dependencies
nsubj(test-6, this-1)
cop(test-6, is-2)
det(test-6, the-3)
amod(test-6, english-4)
compound(test-6, parser-5)
root(ROOT-0, test-6)
```

```
Universal dependencies, enhanced
nsubj(test-6, this-1)
cop(test-6, is-2)
det(test-6, the-3)
amod(test-6, english-4)
compound(test-6, parser-5)
root(ROOT-0, test-6)
```

The output looks quite complex but, in reality, it's not. The output is a list of three major outcomes, where the first is just the POS tags and the parsed tree of the given sentences. The same is plotted in a more elegant way in the following figure. The second is the dependency and positions of the given words. The third is the enhanced version of dependency:

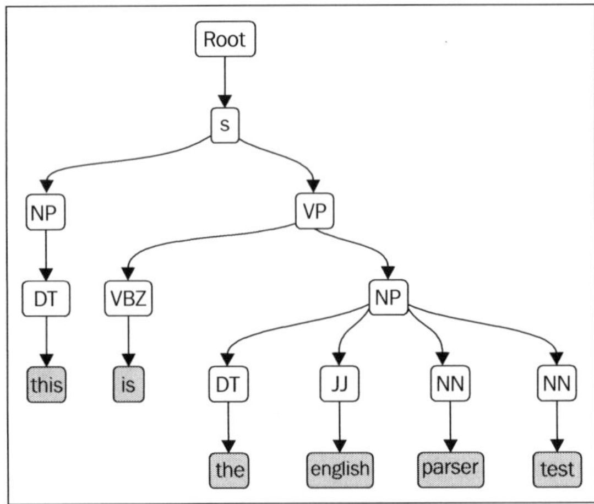

For a better understanding of how to use a Stanford parser, refer to `http://nlpviz.bpodgursky.com/home` and `http://nlp.stanford.edu:8080/parser/index.jsp`.

Chunking

Chunking is shallow parsing where instead of reaching out to the deep structure of the sentence, we try to club some chunks of the sentences that constitute some meaning.

A chunk can be defined as the minimal unit that can be processed. So, for example, the sentence "the President speaks about the health care reforms" can be broken into two chunks, one is "the President", which is noun dominated, and hence is called a **noun phrase (NP)**. The remaining part of the sentence is dominated by a verb, hence it is called a **verb phrase (VP)**. If you see, there is one more sub-chunk in the part "speaks about the health care reforms". Here, one more NP exists that can be broken down again in "speaks about" and "health care reforms", as shown in the following figure:

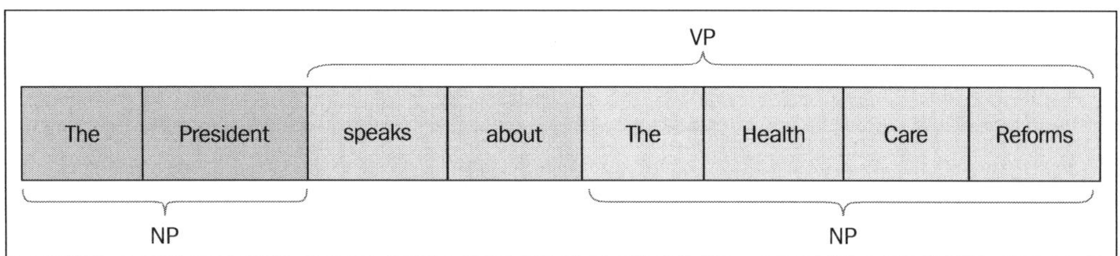

This is how we broke the sentence into parts and that's what we call chunking. Formally, chunking can also be described as a processing interface to identify non-overlapping groups in unrestricted text.

Now, we understand the difference between shallow and deep parsing. When we reach the syntactic structure of the sentences with the help of CFG and understand the syntactic structure of the sentence. Some cases we need to go for semantic parsing to understand the meaning of the sentence. On the other hand, there are cases where, we don't need analysis this deep. Let's say, from a large portion of unstructured text, we just want to extract the key phrases, named entities, or specific patterns of the entities. For this, we will go for shallow parsing instead of deep parsing because deep parsing involves processing the sentence against all the grammar rules and also the generation of a variety of syntactic tree till the parser generates the best tree by using the process of backtracking and reiterating. This entire process is time consuming and cumbersome and, even after all the processing, you might not get the right parse tree. Shallow parsing guarantees the shallow parse structure in terms of chunks which is relatively faster.

So, let's write some code snippets to do some basic chunking:

```
# Chunking
>>>from nltk.chunk.regexp import *
>>>test_sent="The prime minister announced he had asked the chief
government whip, Philip Ruddock, to call a special party room meeting for
9am on Monday to consider the spill motion."
>>>test_sent_pos=nltk.pos_tag(nltk.word_tokenize(test_sent))
>>>rule_vp = ChunkRule(r'(<VB.*>)?(<VB.*>)+(<PRP>)?', 'Chunk VPs')
```

```
>>>parser_vp = RegexpChunkParser([rule_vp],chunk_label='VP')
>>>print parser_vp.parse(test_sent_pos)
>>>rule_np = ChunkRule(r'(<DT>?<RB>?)?<JJ|CD>*(<JJ|CD><,>)*(<NN.*>)+',
'Chunk NPs')
>>>parser_np = RegexpChunkParser([rule_np],chunk_label="NP")
>>>print parser_np.parse(test_sent_pos)
(S
  The/DT
  prime/JJ
  minister/NN
  (VP announced/VBD he/PRP)
  (VP had/VBD asked/VBN)
  the/DT
  chief/NN
  government/NN
  whip/NN
….
….
….
(VP consider/VB)
  the/DT
  spill/NN
  motion/NN
  ./.)

(S
  (NP The/DT prime/JJ minister/NN)                         # 1st noun phrase
  announced/VBD
  he/PRP
  had/VBD
  asked/VBN
  (NP the/DT chief/NN government/NN whip/NN)                  # 2nd noun
phrase
  ,/,
  (NP Philip/NNP Ruddock/NNP)
  ,/,
```

```
  to/TO
  call/VB
  (NP a/DT special/JJ party/NN room/NN meeting/NN)       # 3rd noun
phrase
  for/IN
  9am/CD
  on/IN
  (NP Monday/NNP)                                # 4th noun phrase
  to/TO
  consider/VB
  (NP the/DT spill/NN motion/NN)                           # 5th noun phrase
  ./.)
```

The preceding code is good enough to do some basic chunking of verb and noun phrases. A conventional pipeline in chunking is to tokenize the POS tag and the input string before they are ed to any chunker. Here, we use a regular chunker, as rule NP / VP defines different POS patterns that can be called a verb/noun phrase. For example, the NP rule defines anything that starts with the determiner and then there is a combination of an adverb, adjective, or cardinals that can be chunked in to a noun phrase. Regular expression-based chunkers rely on chunk rules defined manually to chunk the string. So, if we are able to write a universal rule that can incorporate most of the noun phrase patterns, we can use regex chunkers. Unfortunately, it's hard to come up with those kind of generic rules; the other approach is to use a machine learning way of doing chunking. We briefly touched upon `ne_chunk()` and the Stanford NER tagger that both use a pre-trained model to tag noun phrases.

Information extraction

We learnt about taggers and parsers that we can use to build a basic information extraction engine. Let's jump directly to a very basic IE engine and how a typical IE engine can be developed using NLTK.

Any sort of meaningful information can be drawn only if the given input stream goes to each of the following NLP steps. We already have enough understanding of sentence tokenization, word tokenization, and POS tagging. Let's discuss NER and relation extraction as well.

A typical information extraction pipeline looks very similar to that shown in the following figure:

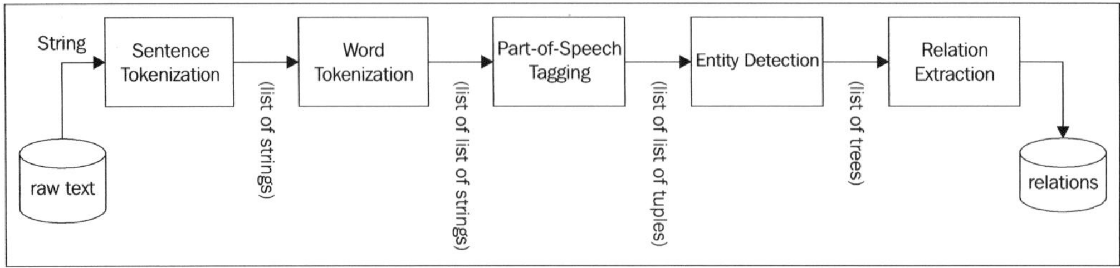

Some of the other preprocessing steps, such as stop word removal and stemming, are generally ignored and do not add any value to an IE engine.

Named-entity recognition (NER)

We already briefly discussed NER generally in the last chapter. Essentially, NER is a way of extracting some of the most common entities, such as names, organizations, and locations. However, some of the modified NER can be used to extract entities such as product names, biomedical entities, author names, brand names, and so on.

Let's start with a very generic example where we are given a text file of the content and we need to extract some of the most insightful named entities from it:

```
# NP chunking (NER)
>>>f=open(# absolute path for the file of text for which we want NER)
>>>text=f.read()
>>>sentences = nltk.sent_tokenize(text)
>>>tokenized_sentences = [nltk.word_tokenize(sentence) for sentence in
sentences]
>>>tagged_sentences = [nltk.pos_tag(sentence) for sentence in tokenized_
sentences]
>>>for sent in tagged_sentences:
>>>print nltk.ne_chunk(sent)
```

In the preceding code, we just followed the same pipeline provided in the preceding figure. We took all the preprocessing steps, such as sentence tokenization, tokenization, POS tagging, and NLTK. NER (pre-trained models) can be used to extract all NERs.

Relation extraction

Relation extraction is another commonly used information extraction operation. Relation extraction as it sound is the process of extracting the different relationships between different entities. There are variety of the relationship that exist between the entities. We have seen relationship like inheritance/synonymous/analogous. The definition of the relation can be dependent on the Information need. For example in the case where we want to look from unstructured text data who is the writer of which book then authorship could be a relation between the author name and book name. With NLTK the idea is to use the same IE pipeline that we used till NER and extend it with a relation pattern based on the NER tags.

So, in the following code, we used an inbuilt corpus of `ieer`, where the sentences are tagged till NER and the only thing we need to specify is the relation pattern we want and the kind of NER we want the relation to define. In the following code, a relationship between an organization and a location has been defined and we want to extract all the combinations of these patterns. This can be applied in various ways, for example, in a large corpus of unstructured text, we will be able to identify some of the organizations of our interest with their corresponding location:

```
>>>import re
>>>IN = re.compile(r'.*\bin\b(?!\b.+ing)')
>>>for doc in nltk.corpus.ieer.parsed_docs('NYT_19980315'):
>>> for rel in nltk.sem.extract_rels('ORG', 'LOC', doc, corpus='ieer', pattern = IN):
>>>print(nltk.sem.rtuple(rel))
[ORG: u'WHYY'] u'in' [LOC: u'Philadelphia']
[ORG: u'McGlashan &AMP; Sarrail'] u'firm in' [LOC: u'San Mateo']
[ORG: u'Freedom Forum'] u'in' [LOC: u'Arlington']
[ORG: u'Brookings Institution'] u', the research group in' [LOC: u'Washington']
[ORG: u'Idealab'] u', a self-described business incubator based in' [LOC: u'Los Angeles']
..
```

Summary

We moved beyond the basic preprocessing steps in this chapter. We looked deeper at NLP techniques, such as parsing and information extraction. We discussed parsing in detail, which parsers are available, and how to use NLTK to do any NLP parsing. You understood the concept of CFG and PCFG and how to learn from a tree bank and build a parser. We talked about shallow and deep parsing and what the difference is between them.

We also talked about some of the information extraction essentials, such as entity extraction and relation extraction. We talked about a typical information extraction engine pipeline. We saw a very small and simple IE engine that can be built in less than 100 lines of code. Think about this kind of system running on an entire Wikipedia dump or an entire web content related to an organization. Cool, isn't it?

We will use some of the topics we've learnt in this chapter in further chapters to build some useful NLP applications.

5
NLP Applications

This chapter discusses NLP applications. Here, we will put all the learning from the previous chapters into action and will see what kind of application can be developed using the concepts we have learned. This will be a complete hands-on chapter. In the last few chapters we have learned most of the preprocessing steps that are required for any NLP application. We know how to use tokenizer, POS tag, and NER and how to perform parsing. This chapter will give you an idea how we can developed some of the complex NLP application using the concepts we have learned.

There are so many applications of NLP in the real world. Some of the most exciting and common examples you can observe are Google Search, Siri, machine translation, Google News, Jeopardy, and spell check. Some of these took many years for researchers to reach this level and bring these applications to their current state. NLP is complicated too; we have seen in the previous chapters that most of the processing steps, such as POS and NER, are still research problems. But with the use of NLTK, we have solved many of these problems with reasonable accuracy. We will not cover the more sophisticated applications such as machine translation or speech recognition in this book. But at this point in time, you should have enough background knowledge to understand some of the basic blocks of these applications. As a NLP enthusiast we should have a basic understanding of these NLP applications. I urge you to try and look for some of these NLP applications on the web and try to understand them.

By the end of this chapter :

- We will introduce reader to few common NLP applications.
- We will develop a NLP application (News summarizer) using what we have learnt so far.
- The importance of different NLP applications and essential details about each of them.

Building your first NLP application

Let's start with one of the very complex NLP applications, which is **summarization**. The concept of summarization is quite simple. We are given an article/passage/story and you will have to generate a summary of the content automatically. Summarization actually requires deep knowledge of NLP because we need to understand not just the structure of the sentence but also the structure of the entire text. We also need to know about genre of the text and the theme of the content.

Since it all looks very complex to us, let's try a very intuitive approach. We will assume that summarization is nothing but ranking of the sentences based on their importance and significance to you. We will create a few rules based on the understanding and the preprocessing tools we have learned so far and will try to come up with an acceptable summary of the news article.

I have scraped an article from the *New York Times* in a text file `nyt.txt`, in the following example. The idea here is to summarize this news article for us. Let's build a version of Google News for our personal use.

To start off, we need to keep in mind that, typically, a sentence that has more entities and nouns has greater importance than other sentences. We will try to normalize the same logic while calculating an **importance score**, using the following code. To get the top-n sentence, we can choose a threshold for the importance score.

Let's read the content of the news article. You can choose any news article with only contents of the news dumped into a text file. The content will look like this:

```
>>>import sys
>>>f=open('nyt.txt','r')
>>>news_content=f.read()
""" President Obama on Monday will ban the federal provision of some
types of military-style equipment to local police departments and sharply
restrict the availability of others, administration officials said.


The ban is part of Mr. Obama's push to ease tensions between law
enforcement and minority communities in reaction to the crises in
Baltimore; Ferguson, Mo.; and other cities.
- - -
blic." It contains dozens of recommendations for agencies throughout the
country."""
```

Once we parse the contents of the news we will need to split the entire news article into a list of sentences. We will go back to our old sentence tokenizer to break the entire news snippet into sentences. Let's also provide some form of sentence number so that we can identify and rank a sentence. Once we have the sentence, we will pass it through a word tokenizer and eventually through the `NER` tagger and `POS` tagger.

```
>>>import nltk
>>>results=[]
>>>for sent_no,sentence in enumerate(nltk.sent_tokenize(news_content)):
>>>     no_of_tokens=len(nltk.word_tokenize(sentence))
>>>     #print no_of_toekns
>>>     # Let's do POS tagging
>>>     tagged=nltk.pos_tag(nltk.word_tokenize(sentence))
>>>     # Count the no of Nouns in the sentence
>>>     no_of_nouns=len([word for word,pos in tagged if pos in
["NN","NNP"] ])
>>>     #Use NER to tag the named entities.
>>>     ners=nltk.ne_chunk(nltk.pos_tag(nltk.word_tokenize(sentence)),
binary=False)
>>>     no_of_ners= len([chunk for chunk in ners if hasattr(chunk,
'node')])
>>>     score=(no_of_ners+no_of_nouns)/float(no_of_toekns)
>>>
>>>     results.append((sent_no,no_of_tokens,no_of_ners,\
no_of_nouns,score,sentence))
```

In the preceding code, we are iterating over a list of sentences calculating a score based on a formula that is nothing but the fraction of tokens being entities as compared to a normal token. We are creating a tuple of all these as the results.

Now, the result is a tuple with all the scores, such as the number of nouns, entities, and so on. We can sort it based on the score in descending order, as shown in the following example:

```
>>>for sent in sorted(results,key=lambda x: x[4],reverse=True):
>>>     print sent[5]
```

Now, the result of this will be sorted by the rank of the sentence. You will be amazed by the kind of results we get for the news article.

Once we have a list of `no_of_nouns` and `no_of_ners` scores, we can actually create some more complex rules around this. For example, a typical news article will start with very important details about the topic, and the last sentence will be a conclusion to the story.

Can we modify the same snippet to incorporate this logic?

The other theory of this kind of summarization is that the important sentences generally contain important words and that most of the the discriminatory words across the corpus will be important. The sentences that has very discriminatory words are important. A very simple measure of that is to calculate the **TF-IDF (term frequency–inverse document frequency)** score of each and every word and then look for an average score normalized by the words that are important; this can then be used as the criteria to choose sentences for our summary.

For explaining the concepts instead of the entire article, just take the first three sentences of the article. Let's see how you can implement something this complex using very few lines of code:

This code require installing scikit. If you have installed anaconda or canopy you should be fine otherwise install scikit using this link.
`scikit-learn.org/0.9/install.html`

```
>>>import nltk
>>>from sklearn.feature_extraction.text import TfidfVectorizer
>>>results=[]
>>>news_content="Mr. Obama planned to promote the effort on Monday during a visit to Camden, N.J. The ban is part of Mr. Obama's push to ease tensions between law enforcement and minority \communities in reaction to the crises in Baltimore; Ferguson, Mo. We are, without a doubt, sitting at a defining moment in American policing, Ronald L. Davis, the director of the Office of Community Oriented Policing Services at the Department of Justice, told reporters in a conference call organized by the White House"


>>>sentences=nltk.sent_tokenize(news_content)


>>>vectorizer = TfidfVectorizer(norm='l2',min_df=0, use_idf=True, smooth_idf=False, sublinear_tf=True)


>>>sklearn_binary=vectorizer.fit_transform(sentences)
>>>print countvectorizer.get_feature_names()
>>>print sklearn_binary.toarray()
>>>for i in sklearn_binary.toarray():
>>>    results.append(i.sum()/float(len(i.nonzero()[0]))
```

In the preceding code, I am using some unknown methods, such as `TfidfVectorizer`, which is a scoring method that will calculate a vector of TF-IDF scores for each sentence in a given list of sentences. Don't worry, we will talk about this in more detail. For this chapter, consider it as a black-box function that, for a given list of sentences/documents, will give you the score corresponding to each sentence and will also provide the ability to build a term-doc matrix that will look just like our output.

We got a dictionary of all the words present across all the sentences and then we have a list of lists where each element assigns each word its individual TF-IDF score. If you got that right, then you can see some of the stop words will get a near-zero score while some discriminatory words like `ban` and `Obama` will get a very high score. Now once we have this in the code, I will look for the average TF-IDF score by using only non-zero TF-IDF words. This will give us a similar kind of score as we got in our first approach.

You will be amazed by the kind of results a simple algorithm can give. I think now you are all set to write your own news summarizer that summarizes any given news article with the two preceding algorithms and the summary will look quite decent. While this kind of approach will give you a decent summarization, it's actually very poor when you compare it with the current state of summarization research. I would recommend looking for some literature relating to summarization. I would also like you to try and combine both the approaches for summarization.

Other NLP applications

Some of the other NLP applications are text classification, machine translation, speech recognition, information retrieval, information extraction, topic segmentation, and discourse analysis. Some of these problems are actually very difficult NLP tasks and a lot of research is still going on in these areas. We will discuss some of these in depth in the next chapter, but as NLP students, we should have a basic understanding of these applications.

Machine translation

The easiest way to understand machine translation is to know how we translate from one language to other. Our mind parses the sentence structure and tries to understand the sentence. Once we understand the sentence, we will try to substitute the words from the original language with those from the target language. While substituting, we use the grammar rules of the target sentence and finally achieve the correct translation.

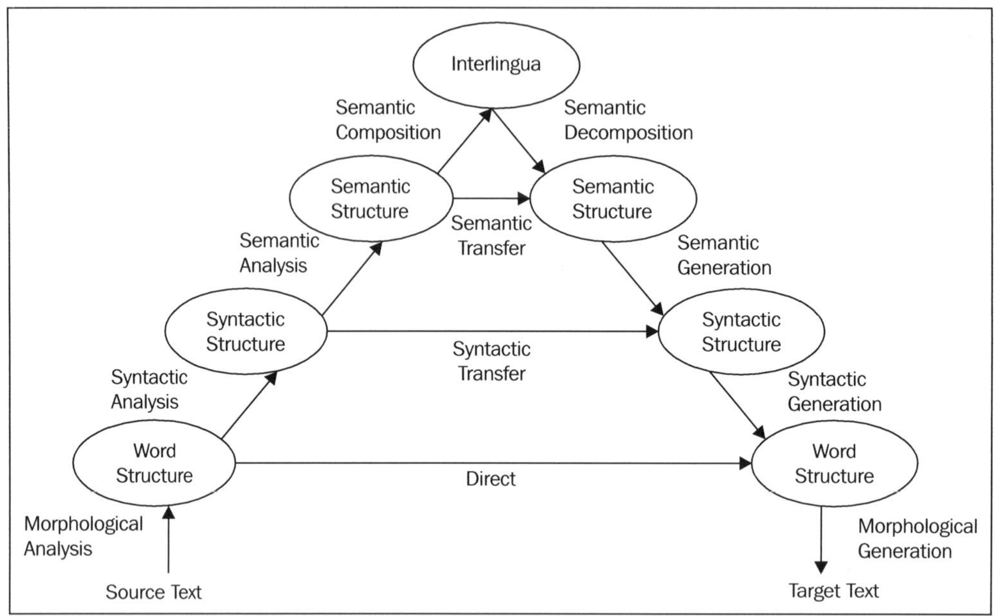

Loosely, the process can be translated to something like the pyramid in the preceding figure. If we start from the source language text, we have to tokenize the sentences that we will parse the tree (for syntactic structure in easy words) to make sure the sentences are correctly formulated. Semantic structure holds the meaning of the sentences, and at the next level, we reach the state of Interlingua, which is an abstract state that is independent from any language. There are multiple ways in which people have developed methods of translation. The more you go on towards the root of the pyramid, the more intense is the NLP processing required. So, based on these levels of transfer, there are a variety of methods that are available. I have listed two of them here:

- **Direct translation**: This will be more of a dictionary-based machine translation while you have huge corpora of source and target language words. This kind of transfer is possible for applications where we have a large corpus of languages available. It's popular because of its simplicity.
- **Syntactic transfer**: Here you will try to build a parser of the source language. There are varieties of ways in which people have approached the problem of parsing. There are deep parsers that actually take care of some parts of semantics too. Once you have a parser, target word substitution happens and the target parser can generate the final sentence in the target language.

Statistical machine translation

Statistical machine translation (**SMT**) is one of the latest approach of machine translation, where people have come up with a variety of ways to apply statistical methods to almost all the aspects of machine translation. The idea behind this kind of algorithm is that we have a huge volume of corpora, parallel text, and language models that can help us predict the language translation in the target language. Google Translate is a great example of SMT, where it learns from the corpora of different language pairs and builds an SMT around it.

Information retrieval

Information retrieval (**IR**) is also one of the most popular and widely used applications. The best exmple of IR is Google Search, where—given an input query from the user—the information retrieval algorithm will try to retrieve the information which is relevant to the user's query.

In simple words, IR is the process of obtaining the most relevant information that is needed by the user. There are a variety of ways in which the information needs can be addressed to the system, but the system eventually retrieves the most relevant infromation.

The way a typical IR system works is that it generates an indexing mechanism, also known as **inverted index**. This is very similar to the indexing schemes used in books, where you will have an index of the words present throughout the book on the last pages of the book. Similarly, an IR system will create an inverted index poslist. A typical posting list will look like this:

```
< Term , DocFreq, [DocId1,DocId2] >
{"the",2 --->[1,2] }
{"US",1 --->[2] }
{"president",2 --->[1,2] }
```

So if any word occurs in both document 1 and document 2, the posting list will be a list of documents pointing to terms. Once you have this kind of data structure, there are different retrieval models that can been introduced. There are different retrieval models that work on different types of data. A few are listed in the following sections.

Boolean retrieval

In the Boolean model, we just need to run a Boolean operation on the poslist. For example, if we are looking for a search query like "US president", the system should look for an intersection of the postlist of "US" and "president".

```
{US}{president}=> [2]
```

Here, the second document turns out to be the relevant document.

Vector space model

The concept of **vector space model (VSM)** derives from geometry. The way to visualize the documents in the high dimension space of vocabulary is to represent it as a vector. So each and every document is represented as a vector in that space. We can represent the vector in various ways, but one of the most useful and efficient ways is using TF-IDF.

Given a term and a corpus, we can calculate the **term frequency (TF)** and **inverse document frequency (IDF)** using the following formula:

$$\mathrm{tf}(t,d) = 0.5 + \frac{0.5 \times \mathrm{f}(t,d)}{\max\{\mathrm{f}(w,d) : w \in d\}}$$

The TF is nothing but the frequency in the document. While the IDF is the inverse of document frequency, which is the count of documents in the corpus where the term occurs:

$$\mathrm{idf}(t,D) = \log \frac{N}{|\{d \in D : t \in d\}|}$$

There are various normalization variants of these, but we can incorporate both of these to create a more robust scoring mechanism to get the scoring of each term in the document. To get to a TF-IDF score, we need to multiply these two scores as follows:

$$\mathrm{tfidf}(t,d,D) = \mathrm{tf}(t,d) \times \mathrm{idf}(t,D)$$

In TF-IDF, we are scoring a term for how much it is present in the current document and how much it is spread across the corpus. This gives us an idea of the terms that are not common across corpora and where ever they are present have a high frequency. It becomes discriminatory to retrieve these documents. We have also used TF-IDF in the previous section, where we describe our summarizer.The same scoring can be used to represent the document as a vector. Once we have all the documents represented in a vectorized form, the vector space model can be formulated.

In VSM, the search query of the user is also considered as a document and represented as a vector. Intuitively, a dot product between these two vectors can be used to get the cosine similarity between the document and the user query.

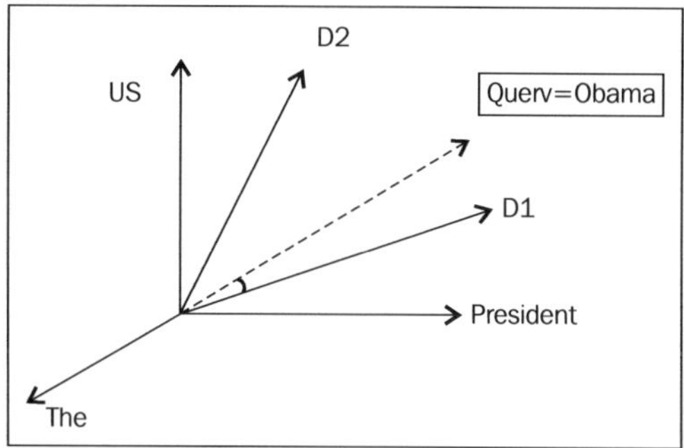

In the preceding diagram, we see that these same documents can be represented using each term as an axis and the query `Obama` will have as much relevance to *D1* as compared to *D2*. The scoring of the query for relevant documents can be formulated as follows:

$$\text{sim}(d_j, q) = \frac{\mathrm{d_j} \cdot \mathrm{q}}{\|\mathrm{d_j}\| \|\mathrm{q}\|} = \frac{\sum_{i=1}^{N} w_{i,j}, w_{i,q}}{\sqrt{\sum_{i=1}^{N} w_{i,j}^2} \sqrt{\sum_{i=1}^{N} w_{i,q}^2}}$$

The probabilistic model

The probabilistic model tries to estimate the probability of the user's need for the document. This model assumes that the probability of the relevance depends on the user query and document representation.The main idea is that a document that is in the relevant set will not be present in the non-relevant set. We denote `dj` as the document and `q` as user query; `R` represents the relevant set of documents, while `P` represents the non-relevant set. The scoring can be done like this:

$$\text{sim}(d_j, q) = \frac{P(R \mid \vec{d}_j)}{P(\overline{R} \mid \vec{d}_j)}$$

For more topics on IR, I would recommend that you read from the following link:

`http://nlp.stanford.edu/IR-book/html/htmledition/irbook.html`

Speech recognition

Speech recognition is a very old NLP problem. People have been trying to address this since the era of World War I, and it still is one of the hottest topics in the area of computing. The idea here is really intuitive. Given the speech uttered by a human can we convert it to text? The problem with speech is that we produce a sequence of sounds, called **phonemes**, that are hard to process, so speech segmentation itself is a big problem. Once the speech is processable, the next step is to go through some of the constraints (models) that are built using training data available. This involves heavy machine learning. If you see the figure representing the modeling as one box of applying constraints, it's actually one of the most complex components of the entire system. While acoustic modeling involves building modes based on phonemes, lexical models will try to address the modeling on smaller segments of sentences, associating a meaning to each segment. Separately language models are built on unigrams and bigrams of words.

Once we build these models, an utterence of the sentences is passed through the process. Once processed for initial preprocessing, the sentence is passed through these acoustic, lexical, and language models for generating the token as output.

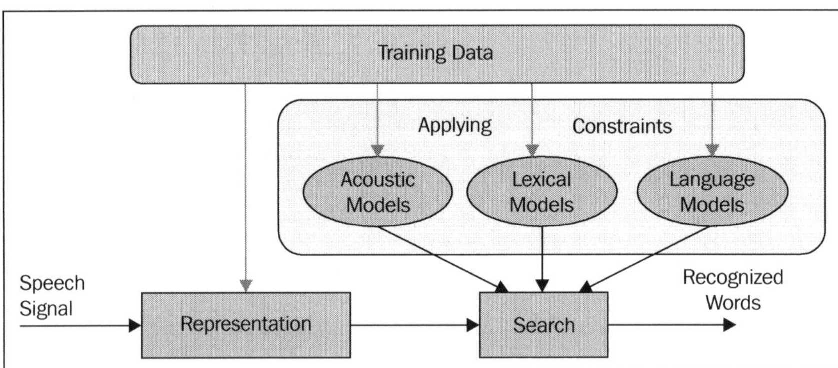

Text classification

Text classification is a very interesting and common application of NLP. In your daily work, you interact with many text classifiers. We use a spam filter, a priority inbox, news aggregators, and so on. All of these are in fact applications built using text classification.

Text classification is a well-defined and somewhat solved problem, and it has been applied across many domains. Typically, any text classification is the process of classifying text documents using words and the combination of words. While it's a typical machine learning problem, many of the preprocessing steps used in text classification are from NLP.

An abstract diagram of text classification is shown here:

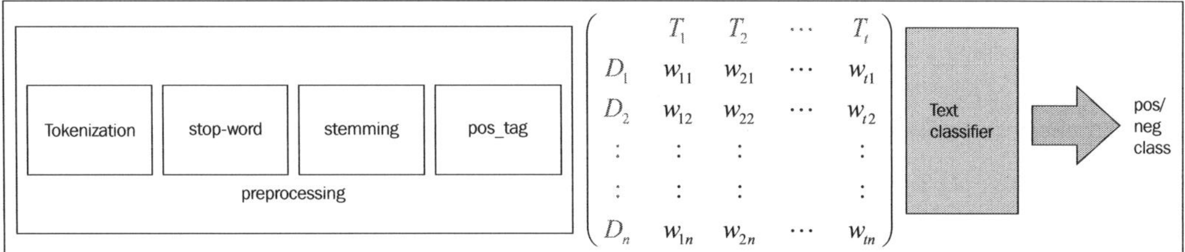

Here we have a bunch of documents for a set of classes. For simplicity, we will use just binary `1/0` as the class. Now let's assume it's a spam detection problem where 1 represents spam and 0 represents normal text which is not to be considered as spam.

The process involves some of the preprocessing steps we learned in previous chapters. While some of these are essential, it depends on the kind of text classification problem we are trying to solve. So in few cases, it's more a case of feature engineering while we drop some of the preprocessing steps. The final goal of feature engineering is to generate a **Term doc matrix** (**TDM**), which holds the vocabulary of the entire corpus: columns and rows are the documents, while the matrix represents a scoring mechanism to show the **Bag of word** (**BOW**) representation. The weighting scheme can be varied to TF, TF-IDF, Bernoulli, and other variations of term frequency.

There are also ways to induce features such as the POS of a given feature, contextual POS, and others, to make our feature space more NLP intense. Once the TDM is generated, the text classification problem becomes a typical supervised/unsupervised classification problem, where given a set of samples, we need to predict what sample belongs to what class. The next chapter is dedicated entirely to this topic. This is definitely a splendid application of NLP/ML and is used quite often for commercial purposes.

Some of the most common use cases in day-to-day scenarios are sentiment analysis, spam classification, e-mail categorization, news categorization, patent classification, and so on. We will talk about text classification in more detail in the next chapter.

Information extraction

Information extraction (**IE**) is a process of extracting meaningful information from unstructured text. IE is yet another widely popular and highly important application. In general, an information extraction engine harnesses huge numbers of unstructured documents and generates some sort of structured/semi-structured **knowledge base** (**KB**) that can be deployed to build an application around it. A simple example is that of generating a very good ontology using a huge set of unstructured text documents. A similar project in this line is DBpedia, where all the Wikipedia articles are used to generate the ontology of artifacts that are interrelated or have some other relationship.

There are mainly two ways of extracting information:

- **Rule-based extraction**: This method is where one uses a template filling mechanism. The idea is to look for some kind predefined use cases for expected outcomes and try to mine the unstructured text for that specific template. For example, building a knowledge base of football will involve getting information on all the players and their profiles, the statistics, some personal information, and so on. All that can be well defined and extracted using either pattern-based rules or POS tags, NERs and relation extraction.
- **Machine learning based**: The other approach involves deeper NLP-based methods such as building a parser specific to the need of our knowledge base. Some of the KBs will require mining the entities that can't be extracted using a pre-trained NER, so we have to build a custom NER. We might want to develop a relation extraction algorithm specific to the KB we are trying to build. This is a more NLP-intensive approach, where we are developing a NLP-based parser or tagger to use for heavy machine learning.

Question answering systems

Question answering (**QA**) systems are intelligent systems that can address any question based on their knowledge base. One of the major examples of this is IBM Watson, which took part in the TV show *Jeopardy* and won over human opponents. A QA system can be broken down to building components from speech recognition for querying the knowledge base while the knowledge base is generated using information retrieval and extraction.

Once you have a question for the system, one big problem is to classify/categorize the question in different ways. The other aspect is to search the knowledge base effectively and retrieve the most precise document. Even after that, we have to generate the answer in a natural way using some of the other applications, such as summarization and parsing.

Dialog systems

Dialog systems are considered the dream application, where given a speech in source language, the system will perform speech recognition and transcribe it to text. This text will then go to a machine translation system that can translate the speech into the target language and then a text-to-speech system will convert it into speech in the target language. This is one of the most desirable applications of NLP, where we can talk to a computer in any language and the computer will reply in the same language. This kind of application can actually destroy the language barrier that exists in the world.

Apple Siri and Google Voice are examples of some of the commercial applications in the line of dialog systems intelligent enough to understand our information needs, try to address them in a set of actions or information, and respond in a human-like manner.

Word sense disambiguation

Word sense disambiguation (**WSD**) is also one of the difficult challenges not solved even after years of research and one of the major causes of application problems, such as question answering, summarization, search, and so on. A simple way to understand the concept is that many words have different meanings when used in different contexts. For example, "cold" in the following example:

- The ice-cream is really cold
- That was cold blooded!

Here the word "cold "has two different senses, and it's really hard for computers to understand this concept. Some of the other NLP processing options, such as `POS` tagging and `NER`, are used to resolve some of these problems.

Topic modeling

Topic modeling, in the context of a large amount of unstructured text content, is really an amazing application, where the primary task is to identify the emerging topics in the corpus and then categorize the documents in the corpus as per these topics. We will discuss this briefly in the next chapter.

Topic modeling uses the same NLP preprocessing, for example, sentence split, tokenization, stemming, and so on. The beauty of the algorithms is that we have an unsupervised way of categorizing the document; also, topics are generated without explicitly mentioning anything prior to the process. I encourage you to look at topic modeling in more detail. Try reading about **latent dirichlet allocation** (**LDA**) and **latent semantics indexing** (**LSI**) for more detail.

Language detection

Given a snippet of text, the detection of language is also a problem. The application of language detection is very important for some of the other NLP applications, such as search, machine translation, speech, and so on. The main concept is learning from the text as features what the language is. A variety of machine learning and NLP techniques are used for feature engineering in the process.

Optical character recognition

Optical character recognition (**OCR**) is an application of NLP and computer vision, where given a handwritten document/ non-digital document, the system can recognize the text and extract it into digital format. This has also been widely researched in the area of machine learning for many years. Some of the big OCR projects are Google Books, where they use OCR to convert non-digital books into a centralized library.

Summary

In conclusion, there are many NLP applications around us that we interact with in our day-to-day routines. NLP is difficult and complex, and some of these problems are still unsolved or do not yet have perfect solutions. So anybody who is looking for problems in NLP, try exploring the literature around that. It's a great time to be an NLP researcher. In the era of Big Data, NLP applications are very popular. Many research labs and organizations are currently working on NLP applications such as speech recognition, search, and text classification.

I believe we have learned a lot up until this chapter. For the next couple of chapters, we will delve deeply into some of the applications described here. We have reached a point where we know enough NLP related preprocessing tools and also have a basic understanding about some of the most popular NLP applications. I hope you leverage some of this learning to build a version of an NLP application.

In the next chapter, we will start with some of the important NLP applications, such as text classification, text clustering, and topic modeling. We will move slightly away from the pure NLTK applications on to how NLTK can be used in conjunction with other libraries.

6
Text Classification

We were talking about some of the most common NLP tools and preprocessing steps in the last chapter. This is the chapter where we will get to use most of the stuff we learnt in the previous chapters, and build one of the most sophisticated NLP applications. We will give you a generic approach about text classification and how you can build a text classifier from scratch with very few lines of code. We will give you a cheat sheet of all the classification algorithms in the context of text classification.

While we will talk about some of the most common text classification algorithms, this is just a brief introduction and to get to a detailed understanding and mathematical background, there are many online resources and books available that you can refer to. We will try to give you all you need to know to get you started with some working code snippets. Text classification is a great use case of NLP, but in this chapter, instead of using NLTK, we will use **scikit-learn** that has a wider range of classification algorithms and its library is much more memory efficient for text mining.

By the end of this chapter:

- You will learn and understand all text classification algorithms
- You will learn end-to-end pipeline to build a text classifier and how to implement it with scikit-learn and NLTK

The following is the scikit-learn cheat sheet for machine learning:

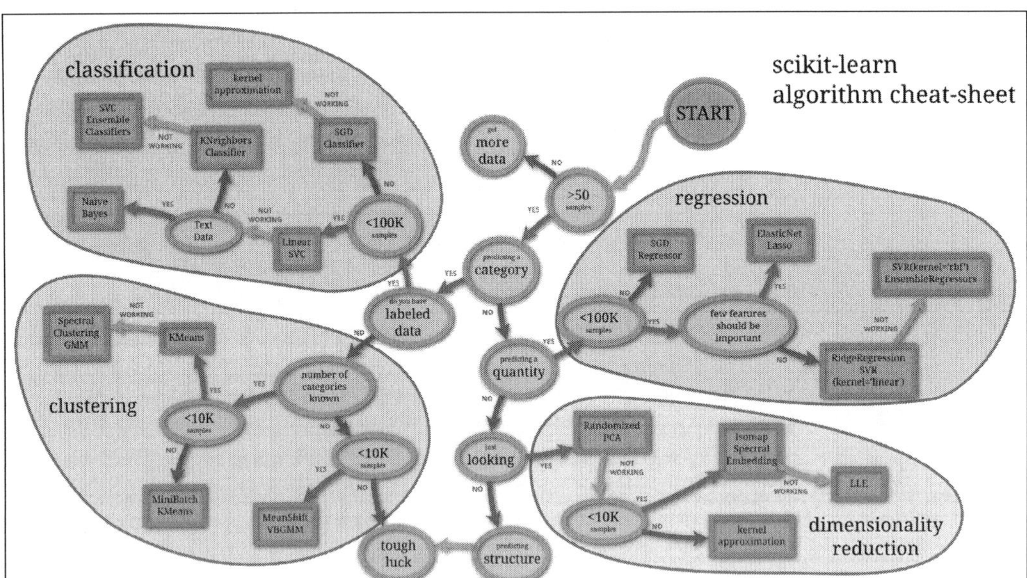

credit : scikit-learn

Now, as you travel along the process shown in the cheat sheet. We have a clear guideline about what kind of algorithm is required for which problem? When we should move from one classifier to another depending on the size of the tagged sample? It's a good place to start following this for building practical application, and in most cases this will work. We will focus mostly on text data while the scikit-learn can work with other types of data as well. We will explore text classification, text clustering, and topic detection in text (**dimensionality reduction**) with examples in this chapter and build some cool NLP applications. I will not go in to more detail about the concepts of machine learning, classification, and clustering in this chapter, as there are enough resources available on the Web for you. We will provide you with more details of all these concepts in the context of a text corpus. Still, let me give you a refresher.

Machine learning

There are two types of machine learning techniques—supervised learning and Unsupervised learning:

- **Supervised learning**: Based on some historic prelabeled samples, machines learn how to predict the future test sample, based on the following categories:

  - **Classification**: This is used when we need to predict whether a test sample belongs to one of the classes. If there are only two classes, it's a binary classification problem; otherwise, it's a multiclass classification.
  - **Regression**: This is used when we need to predict a continuous variable, such as a house price and stock index.
- **Unsupervised learning**: When we don't have any labeled data and we still need to predict the class label, this kind of learning is called unsupervised learning. When we need to group items based on similarity between items, this is called a clustering problem. While if we need to represent high-dimensional data in lower dimensions, this is more of a dimensionality reduction problem.
- **Semi-supervised learning**: This is a class of supervised learning tasks and techniques that also make use of unlabeled data for training. As the name suggests, it's more of a middle ground for supervised and unsupervised learning, where we use small amount of labeled data and large amount of unlabeled data to build a predictive machine learning model.
- **Reinforcement learning**: This is a form of machine learning where an agent can be programmed by a reward and punishment, without specifying how the task is to be achieved.

If you understood the different machine learning algorithms, I want you to guess what kind of machine learning problems the following are:

- You need to predict the values of weather for the next month
- Detection of a fraud in millions of transactions
- Google's priority inbox
- Amazon's recommendations
- Google news
- Self-driving cars

Text classification

The simplest definition of text classification is that it is a classification of text based on the content of that text. Now, in general, all the machine learning methods and algorithms are written for numeric features/variables. One of the most important problems with text corpus is how to represent text as numeric features. There are different transformations prescribed in the literature. Let's start with one of the simplest and most widely used transformations.

Now, to understand the processes of text classification, let's take a real word problem of spams. In the world of WhatsApp and SMS, you get many spam messages. Let's start by solving this real problem of spam detection with the help of text classification. We will be using this running example across the chapter.

Here are a few real examples of SMS's that we asked people to manually tag for us:

```
SMS001 ['spam', 'Had your mobile 11 months or more? U R entitled to Update to the latest colour mobiles with camera for Free! Call The Mobile Update Co FREE on 08002986030']
```

```
SMS002 ['ham', "I'm gonna be home soon and i don't want to talk about this stuff anymore tonight, k? I've cried enough today."]
```

A similar tagged dataset can be downloaded from link here. Make sure you create a CSV like the one show in the example. 'SMSSpamCollection' in the following code which will correspond to this file.

https://archive.ics.uci.edu/ml/datasets/SMS+Spam+Collection

The first thing you want to do here is what we learnt in the last few chapters about data cleaning, tokenization, and stemming to get much cleaner content out of the SMS. I wrote a basic function to clean the text. Let's go over the following code:

```
>>>import nltk
>>>from nltk.corpus import stopwords
>>>from nltk.stem import WordNetLemmatizer
>>>import csv
>>>def preprocessing(text):
>>>     text = text.decode("utf8")
>>>     # tokenize into words
>>>     tokens = [word for sent in nltk.sent_tokenize(text) for word in nltk.word_tokenize(sent)]


>>>     # remove stopwords
>>>     stop = stopwords.words('english')
>>>     tokens = [token for token in tokens if token not in stop]


>>>     # remove words less than three letters
>>>     tokens = [word for word in tokens if len(word) >= 3]
```

```
>>>     # lower capitalization
>>>     tokens = [word.lower() for word in tokens]
>>>     # lemmatize
>>>     lmtzr = WordNetLemmatizer()
>>>     tokens = [lmtzr.lemmatize(word) for word in tokens]
>>>     preprocessed_text= ' '.join(tokens)
>>>     return preprocessed_text
```

We have talked about tokenization, lemmatization, and stop words in *Chapter 3, Part of Speech Tagging*. In the following code, I am just parsing the SMS file and cleaning the content to get cleaner text of the SMS. In the next few lines, I created two lists to get all the cleaned content of the SMS and class label. In **ML** (**Machine learning**) terms all the X and Y:

```
>>>smsdata = open('SMSSpamCollection') # check the structure of this file!
>>>smsdata_data = []
>>>sms_labels = []
>>>csv_reader = csv.reader(sms,delimiter='\t')
>>>for line in csv_reader:
>>>      # adding the sms_id
>>>     sms_labels.append( line[0])
>>>     # adding the cleaned text We are calling preprocessing method
>>>     sms_data.append(preprocessing(line[1]))
>>>sms.close()
```

Before moving any further we need to make sure we have scikit-learn installed on the system.

```
>>>import sklearn
```

If there is an error you made some error installing scikit. Please go to below link and install scikit:

http://scikit-learn.org/stable/install.html

Sampling

Once we have the entire corpus in the form of lists, we need to perform some form of sampling. Typically, the way to sample the entire corpus in development train sets, dev-test sets, and test sets is similar to the sampling shown in the following figure.

The idea behind the whole exercise is to avoid overfitting. If we feed all the data points to the model, then the algorithm will learn from the entire corpus, but the real test of these algorithms is to perform on unseen data. In very simplistic terms, if we are using the entire data in the model learning process the classifier will perform very good on this data, but it will not be robust. The reason being, we have to tune it to perform the best on the given data, but it doesn't learn how to deal with unknown data.

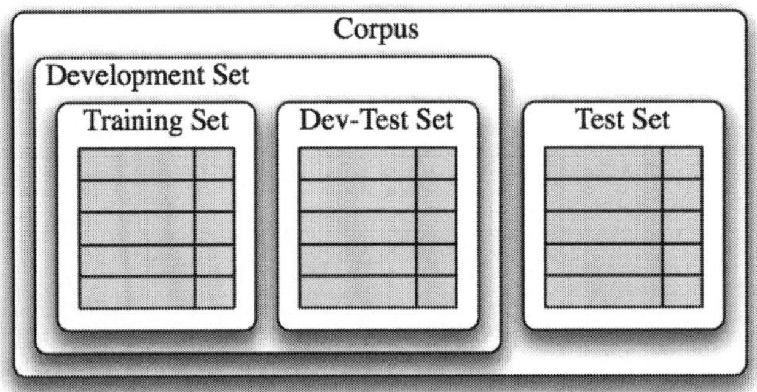

To solve this kind of a problem, the best way is to divide the entire corpus into two major sets. The development set and test set are kept away for the modeling exercise. We just use the dev set to build and tune the model. Once we are done with the entire modeling exercise, the results are projected based on the test set that we put aside. Now, if the model performs well on this set, we are sure that it's accurate and robust for any new data sample.

Sampling itself is a very complicated and well-researched stream in the machine learning community, and it's a remedy for many data **skewness** and overfitting issues. For simplicity, will use the basic sampling, where we just divide the corpus into a split of 70:30:

```
>>>trainset_size = int(round(len(sms_data)*0.70))
>>># i chose this threshold for 70:30 train and test split.
>>>print 'The training set size for this classifier is ' + str(trainset_
size) + '\n'
>>>x_train = np.array([''.join(el) for el in sms_data[0:trainset_size]])
>>>y_train = np.array([el for el in sms_labels[0:trainset_size]])
>>>x_test = np.array([''.join(el) for el in sms_data[trainset_
size+1:len(sms_data)]])
>>>y_test = np.array([el for el in sms_labels[trainset_size+1:len(sms_
labels)]])or el in sms_labels[trainset_size+1:len(sms_labels)]])
>>>print x_train
>>>print y_train
```

- So what do you think will happen if we use the entire data as training data?
- What will happen when we have a very unbalanced sample?

To understand more about the available sampling techniques, go through `http://scikit-learn.org/stable/modules/classes.html#module-sklearn.cross_validation`.

Let's jump to one of the most important things, where we transform the entire text into a vector form. The form is referred to as the **term-document matrix**. If we have to create a term-document matrix for the given example, it will look somewhat like this:

TDM	anymore	call	camera	color	cried	enough	entitled	free	gon	had	latest	mobile
SMS1	0	1	1	1	0	0	1	2	0	1	0	3
SMS2	1	0	0	0	1	1	0	0	1	0	0	0

The representation here of the text document is also known as the **BOW (Bag of Word)** representation. This is one of the most commonly used representation in text mining and other applications. Essentially, we are not considering any context between the words to generate this kind of representation.

To generate a similar term-document matrix in Python, we use scikit vectorizers:

```
>>>from sklearn.feature_extraction.text import CountVectorizer
>>>sms_exp=[ ]
>>>for line in sms_list:
>>>     sms_exp.append(preprocessing(line[1]))
>>>vectorizer = CountVectorizer(min_df=1)
>>>X_exp = vectorizer.fit_transform(sms_exp)
>>>print "||".join(vectorizer.get_feature_names())
>>>print X_exp.toarray()
array([[    1,    0,    1,    1,    1,    0,    0,    1,    2,    0,
1,    0,    1,    3,    1,    0,    0,    0,    1,    0,    0,    2,
0,    0], [    0,    1,    0,    0,    0,    1,    1,    0,    0,    1,
0,    1,    0,    0,    0,    1,    1,    1,    0,    1,    1,    0,
1,    1,    ]])
```

The count vectorizer is a good start, but there is an issue that you will face while using it: longer documents will have higher average count values than shorter documents, even though they might talk about the same topics.

To avoid these potential discrepancies, it suffices to divide the number of occurrences of each word in a document by the total number of words in the document. This new feature is called **tf (Term frequencies)**.

Another refinement on top of tf is to downscale weights for words that occur in many documents in the corpus, and are therefore less informative than those that occur only in a smaller portion of the corpus.

This downscaling is called **tf-idf (term frequency-inverse document frequency)**. Fortunately, scikit also provides a way to achieve the following:

```
>>>from sklearn.feature_extraction.text import TfidfVectorizer
>>>vectorizer = TfidfVectorizer(min_df=2, ngram_range=(1, 2),  stop_
words='english',  strip_accents='unicode',  norm='l2')
>>>X_train = vectorizer.fit_transform(x_train)
>>>X_test = vectorizer.transform(x_test)
```

We now have the text in a matrix format the same as we have in any machine learning exercise. Now, `X_train` and `X_test` can be used for classification using any machine learning algorithm. Let's talk about some of the most commonly used machine learning algorithms in context of text classification.

Naive Bayes

Let's build your first text classifier. Let's start with a Naive Bayes classifier. Naive Bayes relies on the Bayes algorithm and essentially, is a model of assigning a class label to the sample based on the conditional probability class given by features/attributes. Here we deal with frequencies/bernoulli to estimate prior and posterior probabilities.

$$\text{posterior} = \frac{\text{prior} \times \text{likelihood}}{\text{evidence}}.$$

The naive assumption here is that all features are independent of each other, which looks counter intuitive in the case of text. However, surprisingly, Naive Bayes performs quite well in most of the real-world use cases.

Another great thing about NB is that it's too simple and very easy to implement and score. We need to store the frequencies and calculate the probabilities. It's really fast in case of training as well as test (scoring). For all these reasons, in most of the cases of text classification, it serves as a benchmark.

Let's write some code to achieve this classifier:

```
>>>from sklearn.naive_bayes import MultinomialNB
>>>clf = MultinomialNB().fit(X_train, y_train)
>>>y_nb_predicted = clf.predict(X_test)
>>>print y_nb_predicted
```

```
>>>print ' \n confusion_matrix \n '
>>>cm = confusion_matrix(y_test, y_pred)
>>>print cm
>>>print '\n Here is the classification report:'
>>>print classification_report(y_test, y_nb_predicted)
confusion_matrix [[1205 5]
                  [26 156]]
```

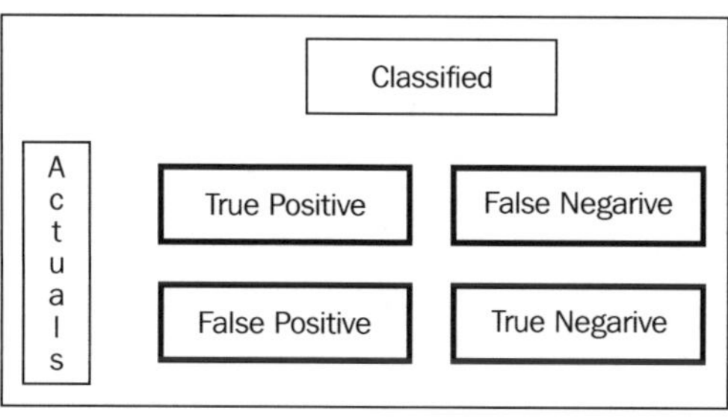

The way to read the confusion matrix is that from all the 1,392 samples in the test set, there were 1205 true positives and 156 true negative cases. However, we also predicted 5 false negatives and 26 false positives. There are different ways of measuring a typical binary classification.

We have given definitions of some of the most common measures used in classification measures:

$$\text{Accuracy} = \frac{tp + tn}{tp + tn + fp + fn}$$

$$\text{Precision} = \frac{tp}{tp + fp}$$

$$\text{Recall} = \frac{tp}{tp + fn}$$

$$F = 2 \cdot \frac{\text{precision} \cdot \text{recall}}{\text{precision} + \text{recall}}$$

Here is the classification report:

```
              Precision    recall    f1-score    support
ham           0.97         1.00      0.98        1210
spam          1.00         0.77      0.87        182
avg / total   0.97         0.97      0.97        1392
```

With the preceding definition, we can now understand the results clearly. So, effectively, all the preceding metrics look good, which means that our classifier is performing accurately, and is robust. I would highly recommend that you look into the module metrics for more options to analyze the results of the classifier. The most important and balanced metric is the `f1` measure (which is nothing but the harmonic mean of precision and recall), which is used widely because it gives a better picture of the coverage and the quality of the classification algorithms. Accuracy intuitively tells us how many true samples have been covered from all the samples. Precision and recall both have significance, while precision talks about how many true positives it got and what else got covered, hand recall gives us details about how accurate we are from the pool of true positives and false negatives.

> For more information on various scikit classes visit the following link:
> `http://scikit-learn.org/stable/modules/classes.html#module-sklearn.metrics`

The other more important process we follow to understand our model is to really look deep into the model by looking at the actual features that contribute to the positive and negative classes. I just wrote a very small snippet to generate the top *n* features and print them. Let's have a look at them:

```
>>>feature_names = vectorizer.get_feature_names()
>>>coefs = clf.coef_
>>>intercept = clf.intercept_
>>>coefs_with_fns = sorted(zip(clf.coef_[0], feature_names))
>>>n = 10
>>>top = zip(coefs_with_fns[:n], coefs_with_fns[:-(n + 1):-1])
>>>for (coef_1, fn_1), (coef_2, fn_2) in top:
>>>     print('\t%.4f\t%-15s\t\t%.4f\t%-15s' % (coef_1, fn_1, coef_2, fn_2))
-9.1602    10 den                    -6.0396    free
-9.1602    15                        -6.3487    txt
-9.1602    1hr                       -6.5067    text
-9.1602    1st ur                    -6.5393    claim
-9.1602    2go                       -6.5681    reply
-9.1602    2marrow                   -6.5808    mobile
-9.1602    2morrow                   -6.5858    stop
-9.1602    2mrw                      -6.6124    ur
-9.1602    2nd innings               -6.6245    prize
-9.1602    2nd ur                    -6.7856    www
```

In the preceding code, I just read all the feature names from the vectorizer, got the coefficients related to the given feature, and then printed the first-10 features. If you want more features, just modify the value of *n*. If we look closely just at the features, we get a lot of information about the model as well as more suggestions about our feature selection and other parameters, such as preprocessing, unigrams/bigrams, stemming, tokenizations, and so on. For example, if you look at the top features of ham you can see that `2morrow`, `2nd innings`, and some of the digits are coming very significantly. We can see on the positive class (spam) term "free" comes out a very significant term which is intuitive while many spam messages will be about some free offers and deal. Some of the other terms to note are prize, www, claim.

For more details, refer to `http://scikitlearn.org/stable/modules/naive_bayes.html`.

Decision trees

Decision trees are one of the oldest predictive modeling techniques, where for the given features and target, the algorithm tries to build a logic tree. There are multiple algorithms that exist for decision trees. One of the most famous and widely used algorithm is **CART**.

CART constructs binary trees using this feature, and constructs a threshold that yields the large amount of information from each node. Let's write the code to get a CART classifier:

```
>>>from sklearn import tree
>>>clf = tree.DecisionTreeClassifier().fit(X_train.toarray(), y_train)
>>>y_tree_predicted = clf.predict(X_test.toarray())
>>>print y_tree_predicted
>>>print ' \n Here is the classification report:'
>>>print classification_report(y_test, y_tree_predicted)
```

The only difference is in the input format of the training set. We need to modify the sparse matrix format to a **NumPy** array because the scikit tree module takes only a NumPy array.

Generally, trees are good when the number of features are very less. So, although our results look good here, people hardly use trees in text classification. On the other hand, trees have some really positive sides to them. It is still one the most intuitive algorithms and is very easy to explain and implement. There are many implementations of tree-based algorithms, such as ID3, C4.5, and C5. scikit-learn uses an optimized version of the CART algorithm.

Stochastic gradient descent

Stochastic gradient descent (**SGD**) is a simple, yet very efficient approach that fits linear models. It is particularly useful when the number of samples (and the number of features) is very large. If you follow the cheat sheet, you will find SGD to be the one-stop solution for many text classification problems. Since it also takes care of regularization and provides different losses, it turns out to be a great choice when experimenting with linear models.

SGD, also known as **Maximum entropy** (**MaxEnt**), provides functionality to fit linear models for classification and regression using different (convex) loss functions and penalties. For example, with loss = log, fits a logistic regression model, while with loss = hinge, it fits a linear support vector machine (SVM).

An example of SGD is as follows:

```
>>>from sklearn.linear_model import SGDClassifier
>>>from sklearn.metrics import confusion_matrix
>>>clf = SGDClassifier(alpha=.0001, n_iter=50).fit(X_train, y_train)
>>>y_pred = clf.predict(X_test)
>>>print '\n Here is the classification report:'
>>>print classification_report(y_test, y_pred)
>>>print ' \n confusion_matrix \n '
>>>cm = confusion_matrix(y_test, y_pred)
>>>print cm
```

Here is the classification report:

	precision	recall	f1-score	support
ham	0.99	1.00	0.99	1210
spam	0.96	0.91	0.93	182
avg / total	0.98	0.98	0.98	1392

Most informative features:

```
    -1.0002    sir                    2.3815    ringtoneking
    -0.5239    bed                    2.0481    filthy
    -0.4763    said                   1.8576    service
    -0.4763    happy                  1.7623    story
    -0.4763    might                  1.6671    txt
    -0.4287    added                  1.5242    new
    -0.4287    list                   1.4765    ringtone
    -0.4287    morning                1.3813    reply
```

-0.4287	always	1.3337	message
-0.4287	and	1.2860	call
-0.4287	plz	1.2384	chat
-0.3810	people	1.1908	text
-0.3810	actually	1.1908	real
-0.3810	urgnt	1.1431	video

Logistic regression

Logistic regression is a linear model for classification. It's also known in the literature as logit regression, maximum-entropy classification (MaxEnt), or the log-linear classifier. In this model, the probabilities describing the possible outcomes of a single trial are modeled using a logit function.

As an optimization problem, the `L2` binary class' penalized logistic regression minimizes the following cost function:

$$\min_{w,c} \frac{1}{2} w^T w + C \sum_{i=1}^{n} \log\left(\exp\left(-y_i\left(X_i^T w + c\right)\right) + 1\right)$$

Similarly, `L1` the binary class' regularized logistic regression solves the following optimization problem:

$$\min_{w,c} \frac{1}{2} \|w\|_1 + C \sum_{i=1}^{n} \log\left(\exp\left(-y_i\left(X_i^T w + c\right)\right) + 1\right)$$

Support vector machines

Support vector machines (SVM) is currently the-state-of-art algorithm in the field of machine learning.

SVM is a non-probabilistic classifier. SVM constructs a set of hyperplanes in an infinite-dimensional space, which can be used for classification, regression, or other tasks. Intuitively, a good separation is achieved by a hyperplane that has the largest distance to the nearest training data point of any class (the so-called functional margin), since in general, the larger the margin, the lower the size of classifier.

Let's build one of the most sophisticated supervised learning algorithms with scikit:

```
>>>from sklearn.svm import LinearSVC
>>>svm_classifier = LinearSVC().fit(X_train, y_train)
>>>y_svm_predicted = svm_classifier.predict(X_test)
>>>print '\n Here is the classification report:'
>>>print classification_report(y_test, y_svm_predicted)
>>>cm = confusion_matrix(y_test, y_pred)
>>>print cm
```

Here is the classification report for the same:

```
             precision    recall  f1-score   support

        ham       0.99      1.00      0.99      1210
       spam       0.97      0.90      0.93       182
avg / total       0.98      0.98      0.98      1392


confusion_matrix  [[1204    6] [  17  165]]
```

The most informative features:

```
    -0.9657    road                    2.3724    txt
    -0.7493    mail                    2.0720    claim
    -0.6701    morning                 2.0451    service
    -0.6691    home                    2.0008    uk
    -0.6191    executive               1.7909    150p
    -0.5984    said                    1.7374    www
    -0.5978    lol                     1.6997    mobile
    -0.5876    kate                    1.6736    50
    -0.5754    got                     1.5882    ringtone
    -0.5642    darlin                  1.5629    video
    -0.5613    fullonsms               1.4816    tone
    -0.5613    fullonsms com           1.4237    prize
```

These are definitely the best results so far from all the supervised algorithms we have tried. Now with this, I will stop with supervised classifiers. There are millions of books available related to the different machine learning algorithms; even for individual algorithms, there are many books that are available for you. I would highly recommend you to have a deep understanding of any of the preceding algorithms before you use them for any of the real-world applications.

The Random forest algorithm

A random forest is an ensemble classifier that estimates based on the combination of different decision trees. Effectively, it fits a number of decision tree classifiers on various subsamples of the dataset. Also, each tree in the forest built on a random best subset of features. Finally, the act of enabling these trees gives us the best subset of features among all the random subsets of features. Random forest is currently one of best performing algorithms for many classification problems.

An example of Random forest is as follows:

```
>>>from sklearn.ensemble import RandomForestClassifier
>>>RF_clf = RandomForestClassifier(n_estimators=10)
>>>predicted = RF_clf.predict(X_test)
>>>print '\n Here is the classification report:'
>>>print classification_report(y_test, predicted)
>>>cm = confusion_matrix(y_test, y_pred)
>>>print cm
```

People who still want to work with NLTK for text classification. Please go through the following link:

`http://www.nltk.org/howto/classify.html`

Text clustering

The other family of problems that can come with text is unsupervised classification. One of the most common problem statements you can get is "I have these millions of documents (unstructured data). Is there a way I can group them into some meaningful categories?". Now, once you have some samples of tagged data, we could build a supervised algorithm that we talked about, but here, we need to use an unsupervised way of grouping text documents.

Text clustering is one of the most common ways of unsupervised grouping, also known as, clustering. There are a variety of algorithms available using clustering. I mostly used **k-means** or **hierarchical** clustering. I will talk about both of them and how to use them with a text corpus.

K-means

Very intuitively, as the name suggest, we are trying to find k groups around the mean of the data points. So, the algorithm starts with picking up some random data points as the centroid of all the data points. Then, the algorithm assigns all the data points to it's nearest centroid. Once this iteration is done, recalculation of the centroid happens and these iterations continue until we reach a state where the centroids don't change (algorithm saturate).

There is a variant of the algorithm that uses mini batches to reduce the computation time, while still attempting to optimize the same objective function.

Mini batches are subsets of the input data randomly sampled in each training iteration. These options should always be tried once your dataset is really huge and you want less training time.

An example of K-means is as follows:

```
>>>from sklearn.cluster import KMeans, MiniBatchKMeans
>>>true_k=5
>>>km = KMeans(n_clusters=true_k, init='k-means++', max_iter=100, n_
init=1)
>>>kmini = MiniBatchKMeans(n_clusters=true_k, init='k-means++', n_init=1,
init_size=1000, batch_size=1000, verbose=opts.verbose)
>>># we are using the same test,train data in TFIDF form as we did in
text classification
>>>km_model=km.fit(X_train)
>>>kmini_model=kmini.fit(X_train)
>>>print "For K-mean clustering "
>>>clustering = collections.defaultdict(list)
>>>for idx, label in enumerate(km_model.labels_):
>>>        clustering[label].append(idx)
>>>print "For K-mean Mini batch clustering "
>>>clustering = collections.defaultdict(list)
>>>for idx, label in enumerate(kmini_model.labels_):
>>>        clustering[label].append(idx)
```

In the preceding code, we just imported scikit-learn's `kmeans` / `minibatchkmeans` and fitted the same training data that we were using in the running examples. We can also print a cluster for each sample using the last three lines of the code.

Topic modeling in text

The other famous problem in the context of the text corpus is finding the topics of the given document. The concept of topic modeling can be addressed in many different ways. We typically use **LDA** (**Latent Dirichlet allocation**) and LSI (Latent semantic indexing) to apply topic modeling text documents.

Typically, in most of the industries, we have huge volumes of unlabeled text documents. In case of an unlabeled corpus to get the initial insights of the corpus, a topic model is a great option, as it not only gives us topics of relevance, but also categorizes the entire corpus into number of topics given to the algorithm.

We will use a new Python library "gensim" that implements these algorithms for us. So, let's jump to the implementation of LDA and LSI for the same running SMS dataset. Now, the only change to the problem is that we want to model different topics in the SMS data and also want to know which document belongs to which topic. A better and more realistic use case could be to run topic modeling on the entire Wikipedia dump to find different kinds of topics that have been discussed there, or to run topic modeling on billions of reviews/complaints from customers to get an insight of the topics that people discuss.

Installing gensim

One of the easiest ways to install gensim is using a package manager:

```
>>>easy_install -U gensim
```

Otherwise, you can install it using:

```
>>>pip install gensim
```

Once you're done with the installation, run the following command:

```
>>>import gensim
```

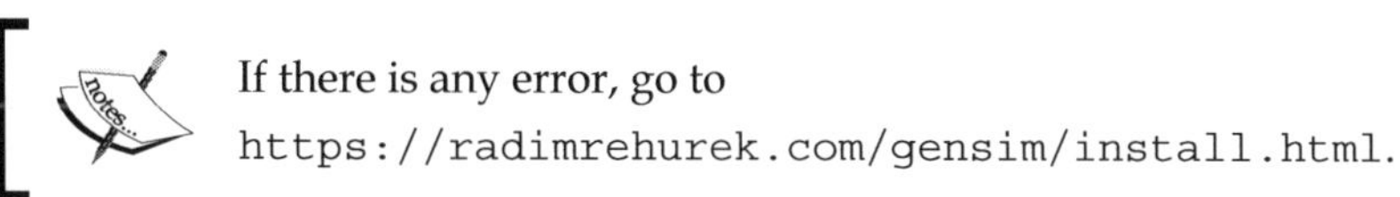

If there is any error, go to https://radimrehurek.com/gensim/install.html.

Now, let's look at the following code:

```
>>>from gensim import corpora, models, similarities
>>>from itertools import chain
>>>import nltk
```

```
>>>from nltk.corpus import stopwords
>>>from operator import itemgetter
>>>import re
>>>documents = [document for document in sms_data]
>>>stoplist = stopwords.words('english')
>>>texts = [[word for word in document.lower().split() if word not in
stoplist] \ for document in documents]
```

We are just reading the document in our SMS data and removing the stop words. We could use the same method that we did in the previous chapters to do this. Here, we are using a library-specific way of doing things.

> Gensim has all the typical NLP features as well provides some great way to create different corpus formats, such as TFIDF, libsvm, market matrix. It also provides conversion of one to another.

In the following code, we are converting the list of documents to a BOW model and then, to a typical **TF-IDF** corpus:

```
>>>dictionary = corpora.Dictionary(texts)
>>>corpus = [dictionary.doc2bow(text) for text in texts]
>>>tfidf = models.TfidfModel(corpus)
>>>corpus_tfidf = tfidf[corpus]
```

Once you have a corpus in the required format, we have the following two methods, where given the number of topics, the model tries to take all the documents from the corpus to build a LDA/LSI model:

```
>>>si = models.LsiModel(corpus_tfidf, id2word=dictionary, num_topics=100)
>>>#lsi.print_topics(20)
>>>n_topics = 5
>>>lda = models.LdaModel(corpus_tfidf, id2word=dictionary, num_topics=n_
topics)
```

Once the model is built, we need to understand the different topics, what kind of terms represent that topic, and we need to print some top terms related to that topic:

```
>>>for i in range(0, n_topics):
>>>        temp = lda.show_topic(i, 10)
>>>        terms = []
>>>        for term in temp:
>>>            terms.append(term[1])
>>>            print "Top 10 terms for topic #" + str(i) + ": "+ ", ".join(terms)
Top 10 terms for topic #0: week, coming, get, great, call, good, day, txt, like, wish
Top 10 terms for topic #1: call, ..., later, sorry, 'll, lor, home, min, free, meeting
Top 10 terms for topic #2: ..., n't, time, got, come, want, get, wat, need, anything
Top 10 terms for topic #3: get, tomorrow, way, call, pls, 're, send, pick, ..., text
Top 10 terms for topic #4: ..., good, going, day, know, love, call, yup, get, make
```

Now, if you look at the output, we have five different topics with clearly different intent. Think about the same exercise for Wikipedia or a huge corpus of web pages, and you will get some meaningful topics that represent the corpus.

References

- http://scikit-learn.org/
- https://radimrehurek.com/gensim/
- https://en.wikipedia.org/wiki/Document_classification

Summary

The idea behind this chapter was to introduce you to the world of text mining. We want to give you a basic introduction to some of the most common algorithms available with text classification and clustering .We know how some of these concept will help you to build really great NLP applications, such as spam filters, domain centric news feeds, web page taxonomy, and so on. Though we have not used NLTK to classify the module in our code snippets, we used NLTK for all the preprocessing steps. We highly recommend you to use scikit-learn over NLTK for any classification problem. In this chapter, we started with machine learning and the types of problems that it can address. We discussed some of the specifics of ML problems in the context of text. We talked about some of the most common classification algorithms that are used for text classification, clustering, and topic modeling. We also give you enough implementation details to get the job done. I still think you need to read a lot about each and every algorithm separately to understand the theory and to gain in-depth understanding of them.

We also provided you an entire pipeline of the process that you need to follow in case of any text mining problem. We covered most of the practical aspects of machine learning, such as sampling, preprocessing, model building, and model evaluation.

The next chapter will also not be directly related to NLTK/NLP, but it will be a great tool for a data scientist/NLP enthusiast. In most of NLP problems, we deal with unstructured text data, and the Web is one of the richest and biggest data sources available for this. Let's learn how to gather data from the Web and how to efficiently use it to build some amazing NLP applications.

7

Web Crawling

The largest repository of unstructured text is the Web, and if you know how to crawl it, then you have all the data you need readily available for your experiments. Hence, web crawling is something worth learning for people who are interested in NLTK. This chapter is all about gathering data from the Web.

In this chapter we will use an amazing Python library called **Scrapy** to write our web crawlers. We will provide you all the details to configure different settings that are required. We will write some of the most common spider strategies and many use cases. Scrapy also requires some understanding about **XPath**, crawling, scraping, and some concepts related to the Web in general. We will touch upon these topics and make sure you understand their practical aspects, before really getting in to their implementation. By the end of this chapter, you will have a better understand of web crawler.

- How we can write our own crawler using Scrapy
- Understanding about all the major Scrapy functionality

Web crawlers

One of the biggest web crawler is Google that crawls the entire **World Wide Web (WWW)**. Google has to traverse every page that exists on the Web and scrape/crawl the entire content.

A web crawler is a computer program that systematically browses the web page by page and also scrapes/crawls the content of the pages. A web crawler can also parse the next set of URLs to be visited from the crawled content. So, if these processes run indefinitely over the entire Web, we can crawl through all the web pages. Web crawlers are interchangeably also called spiders, bots, and scrapers. They all mean the same.

There are a few main points we need to think about before writing our first crawler. Now, every time a web crawler traverses a page, we must decide what kind of content we want to select and what content we want to ignore. For applications such as a search engine, we should ignore all the images, js files, css files, and other files and should concentrate only on HTML content that can be indexed and exposed to the search. In some information extraction engines, we select specific tags or parts of a web page. We also need to extract the URLs if we want to do the crawling recursively. This brings us to the topic of crawling strategy. Here, we need to decide whether we want to go recursively in depth first manner or breadth first manner. We want to follow all the URLs on the next page and then go in depth first manner till we get the URLs, or we should go to all the URLs in the next page and do this recursively.

We also need to make sure that we are not going in the self loop stage because essentially, we traverse a graph in most of the cases. We need to make sure we have a clear revisit strategy for a page. One of the most talked about crawled policies is focused crawling, where we know what kind of domains/topics we are looking for, and the ones that need to be crawled. Some of these issues will be discussed in more detail in the spider section.

Take a look at the video on Udacity at `https://www.youtube.com/watch?v=CDXOcvUNBaA`.

Writing your first crawler

Let's start with a very basic crawler that will crawl the entire content of a web page. To write the crawlers, we will use Scrapy. Scrapy is a one of the best crawling solutions using Python. We will explore all the different features of Scrapy in this chapter. First, we need to install Scrapy for this exercise.

To do this, type in the following command:

```
$ pip install scrapy
```

This is the easiest way of installing Scrapy using a package manager. Let's now test whether we got everything right or not. (Ideally, Scrapy should now be part of `sys.path`):

```
>>>import scrapy
```

If there is any error, then take a look at http://doc.scrapy.org/en/latest/intro/install.html.

At this point, we have Scrapy working for you. Let's start with an example spider app with Scrapy:

```
$ scrapy startproject tutorial
```

Once you write the preceding command, the directory structure should look like the following:

```
tutorial/
    scrapy.cfg   #the project configuration file
    tutorial/       #the project's python module, you'll later import
your code from here.
        __init__.py
        items.py          #the project's items file.
        pipelines.py    #the project's pipelines file.
        settings.py      # the project's settings file.
        spiders/   #a directory where you'll later put your spiders.
              __init__.py
```

The top folder will be given the name of the example tutorial in this case. Then, there is the project configuration file (scrapy.cfg) that will define the kind of setting file that should be used for the project. It also provides the deploy URLs for the project.

Another important part of tutorial setting.py is where we can decide what kind of item pipeline and spider will be used. The item.py and pipline.py are the files that define the data and kind of preprocessing we need to do on the parsed item. The spider folder will contain the different spiders you wrote for the specific URLs.

For our first test spider, we will dump the contents of a news in a local file. We need to create a file named NewsSpider.py, and put it in the path /tutorial/spiders. Let's write the first spider:

```
>>>from scrapy.spider import BaseSpider
>>>class NewsSpider(BaseSpider):
>>>     name = "news"
>>>     allowed_domains = ["nytimes.com"]
>>>     start_URLss = [
```

```
>>>         'http://www.nytimes.com/'
>>>     ]
>>>def parse(self, response):
>>>         filename = response.URLs.split("/")[-2]
>>>         open(filename, 'wb').write(response.body)
```

Once we have this spider ready, we can start crawling using the following command:

```
$ scrapy crawl news
```

After you enter the preceding command, you should see some logs like this:

```
[scrapy] INFO: Scrapy 0.24.5 started (bot: tutorial)
[scrapy] INFO: Optional features available: ssl, http11, boto
[scrapy] INFO: Overridden settings: {'NEWSPIDER_MODULE': 'tutorial.
spiders', 'SPIDER_MODULES': ['tutorial.spiders'], 'BOT_NAME': 'tutorial'}
[scrapy] INFO: Enabled extensions: LogStats, TelnetConsole, CloseSpider,
WebService, CoreStats, SpiderState
```

If you don't see logs like the ones shown in the preceding snippet, you have missed something. Check the location of the spider and other Scrapy-related settings, such as the name of the spider matching to the crawl command, and whether `setting.py` is configured for the same spider and item pipeline or not.

Now, if you are successful, there should be a file in your local folder with the name `www.nytimes.com` that has the entire web content of the `www.nytimes.com` page.

Let's see some of the terms that we used in the spider code in more detail:

- `name`: This is the name of the spider that works as an identifier for Scrapy to look for the `spider` class. So, the crawl command argument and this name should always match. Also make sure that it's unique and case sensitive.
- `start_urls`: This is a list of URLs where the spider will begin to crawl. The crawler with start from a seed URL and using the `parse()` method, it will parse and look for the next URL to crawl. Instead of just a single seed URL, we can provide a list of URLs that can start the crawl.
- `parse()`: This method is called to parse the data from start URLs. The logic of what kind of element is to be selected for specific attributes of item. This could be as simple as dumping the entire content of HTML to as complex as many parse methods callable from parse, and different selectors for individual item attributes.

So, the code does nothing but starts with the given URLs (in this case, `www.nytimes.com`) and crawls the entire content of the page. Typically, a crawler is more complex and will do much more than this; now, let's take a step back and understand what happened behind the scenes. For this, take a look at the following figure:

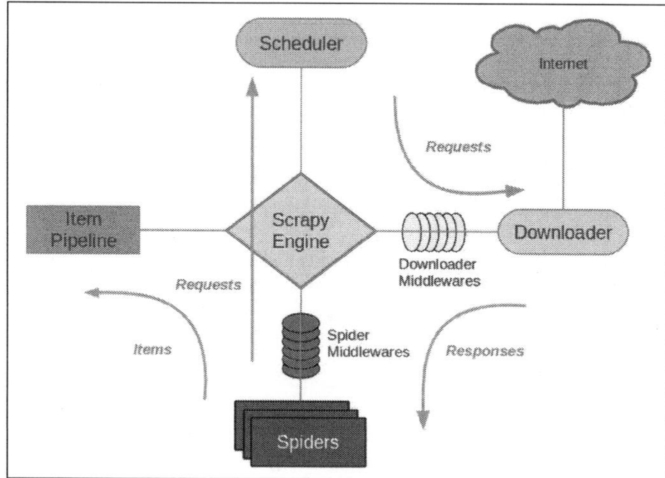

credit :Scrapy

Data flow in Scrapy

The data flow in Scrapy is controlled by the execution engine and goes like this:

1. The process starts with locating the chosen spider and opening the first URL from the list of `start_urls`.
2. The first URL is then scheduled as a request in a scheduler. This is more of an internal to Scrapy.
3. The Scrapy engine then looks for the next set of URLs to crawl.
4. The scheduler then sends the next URLs to the engine and the engine then forwards it to the downloader using the downloaded middleware. These middlewares are where we place different proxies and user-agent settings.
5. The downloader downloads the response from the page and passes it to the spider, where the parse method selects specific elements from the response.
6. Then, the spider sends the processed item to the engine.
7. The engine sends the processed response to the item pipeline, where we can add some post processing.
8. The same process continues for each URL until there are no remaining requests.

The Scrapy shell

The best way to understand Scrapy is to use it through a shell and to get your hands dirty with some of the initial commands and tools provided by Scrapy. It allows you to experiment and develop your XPath expressions that you can put into your spider code.

> To experiment with the Scrapy shell, I would recommend you to install one of the developer tools (**Chrome**) and Firebug (**Mozilla Firefox**) as a plugin. This tool will help us dig down to the very specific part that we want from the web page.

Now, let's start with a very interesting use case where we want to capture the trending topics from Google news (`https://news.google.com/`).

The steps to follow here are:

1. Open `https://news.google.com/` in your favorite browser.
2. Go to the trending topic section on Google news. Then, right-click on and select **Inspect Element** for the first topic, as shown in the following screenshot:

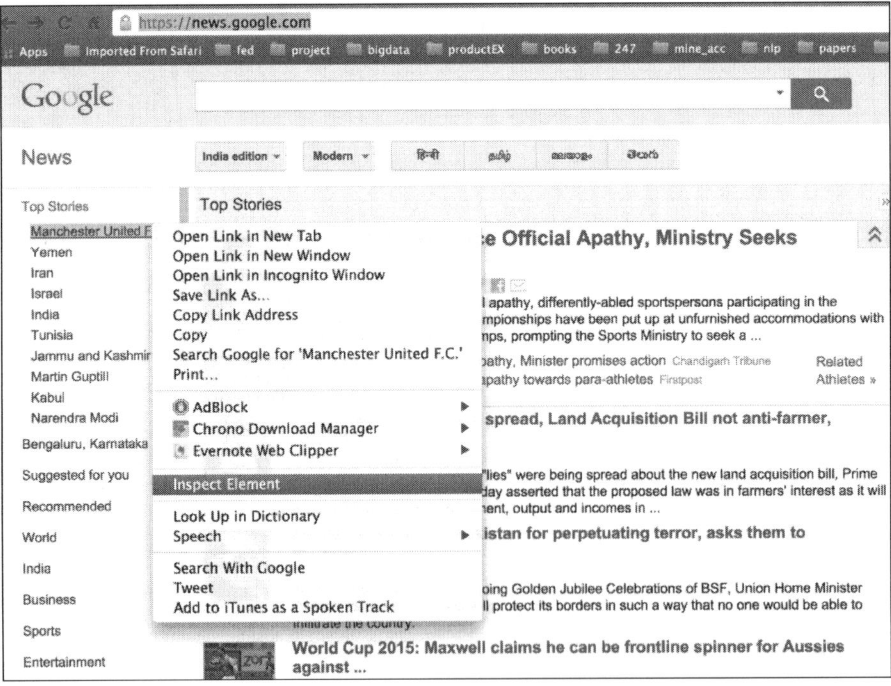

3. The moment you open this, there will be a side window that will pop up and you will get a view.
4. Search and select the `div` tag. For this example, we are interested in `<div class="topic">`.
5. Once this is done, you will come to know that we have actually parsed the specific part of the web page, as shown in the following screenshot:

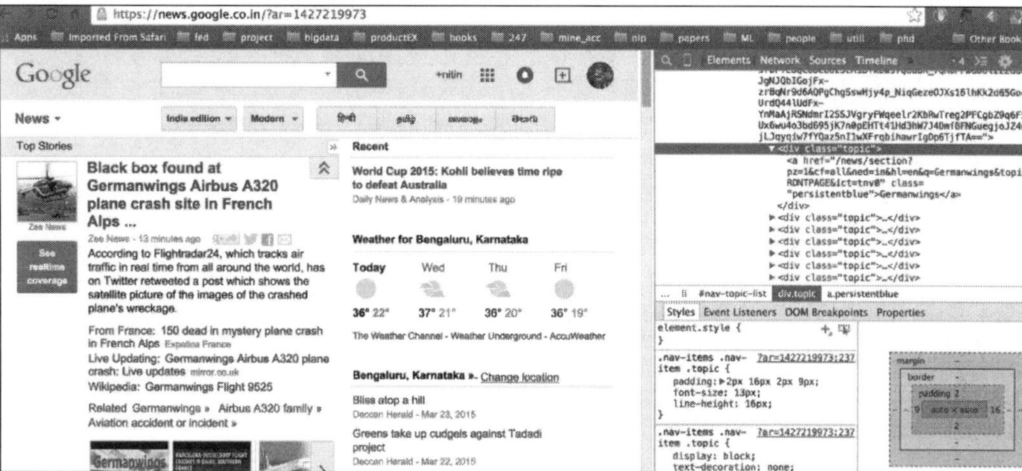

Now, what we actually did manually in the preceding steps can be done in an automated way. Scrapy uses an XML path language called XPath. XPath can be used to achieve this kind of functionality. So, let's see how we can implement the same example using Scrapy.

To use Scrapy, put the following command in you cmd:

```
$scrapy shell https://news.google.com/
```

The moment you hit enter, the response of the Google news page is loaded in the Scrapy shell. Now, let's move to the most important aspect of Scrapy where we want to understand how to look for a specific HTML element of the page. Let's start and run the example of getting topics from Google news that are shown in the preceding image:

```
In [1]: sel.xpath('//div[@class="topic"]').extract()
```

The output to this will be as follows:

```
Out[1]:
[<Selector xpath='//div[@class="topic"]' data=u'<div class="topic"><a
href="/news/sectio'>,
<Selector xpath='//div[@class="topic"]' data=u'<div class="topic"><a
href="/news/sectio'>,
<Selector xpath='//div[@class="topic"]' data=u'<div class="topic"><a
href="/news/sectio'>]
```

Now, we need to understand some of the functions that Scrapy and XPath provide to experiment with the shell and then, we need to update our spider to do more sophisticated stuff. Scrapy selectors are built with the help of the lxml library, which means that they're very similar in terms of speed and parsing accuracy.

Let's have a look at some of the most frequently used methods provided for selectors:

- `xpath()`: This returns a list of selectors, where each of the selectors represents the nodes selected by the XPath expression given as an argument.
- `css()`: This returns a list of selectors. Here, each of the selectors represent the nodes selected by the CSS expression given as an argument.
- `extract()`:This returns content as a string with the selected data.
- `re()`: This returns a list of unicode strings extracted by applying the regular expression given as an argument.

I am giving you a cheat sheet of these top 10 selector patterns that can cover most of your work for you. For a more complex selector, if you search the Web, there should be an easy solution that you can use. Let's start with extracting the title of the web page that is very generic for all web pages:

```
In [2] :sel.xpath('//title/text()')
Out[2]: [<Selector xpath='//title/text()' data=u' Google News'>]
```

Now, once you have selected any element, you also want to extract for more processing. Let's extract the selected content. This is a generic method that works with any selector:

```
In [3]: sel.xpath('//title/text()').extract()
Out[3]: [u' Google News']
```

The other very generic requirement is to look for all the elements in the given page. Let's achieve this with this selector:

```
In [4]: sel.xpath('//ul/li')
Out [4] : list of elements (divs and all)
```

We can extract all the titles in the page with this selector:

```
In [5]: sel.xpath('//ul/li/a/text()').extract()
Out [5]: [ u'India',
u'World',
u'Business',
u'Technology',
u'Entertainment',
u'More Top Stories']
```

With this selector, you can extract all the hyperlinks in the web page:

```
In [6]:sel.xpath('//ul/li/a/@href').extract()
Out [6] : List of urls
```

Let's select all the `<td>` and `div` elements:

```
In [7]:sel.xpath('td'')
In [8]:divs=sel.xpath("//div")
```

This will select all the `divs` elements and then, you can loop it:

```
In [9]: for d in divs:
    printd.extract()
```

This will print the entire content of each div in the entire page. So, in case you are not able to get the exact div name, you can also look at the regex-based search.

Now, let's select all `div` elements that contain the attribute `class="topic"`:

```
In [10]:sel.xpath('/div[@class="topic"]').extract()
In [11]:  sel.xpath("//h1").extract()          # this includes the h1 tag
```

This will select all the `<p>` elements in the page and get the class of those elements:

```
In [12 ] for node in sel.xpath("//p"):
print node.xpath("@class").extract()
Out[12] print all the <p>
```

```
In [13]: sel.xpath("//li[contains(@class, 'topic')]")

Out[13]:

[<Selector xpath="//li[contains(@class, 'topic')]" data=u'<li class="nav-item nv-FRONTPAGE selecte'>,

<Selector xpath="//li[contains(@class, 'topic')]" data=u'<li class="nav-item nv-FRONTPAGE selecte'>]
```

Let's write some selector nuggets to get the data from a css file. If we just want to extract the title from the css file, typically, everything works the same, except you need to modify the syntax:

```
In [14] :sel.css('title::text').extract()

Out[14]: [u'Google News']
```

Use the following command to list the names of all the images used in the page:

```
In[15]: sel.xpath('//a[contains(@href, "image")]/img/@src').extract()

Out [15] : Will list all the images if the web developer has put the images in /img/src
```

Let's see a regex-based selector:

```
In [16 ]sel.xpath('//title').re('(\w+)')

Out[16]: [u'title', u'Google', u'News', u'title']
```

In some cases, removing the namespaces can help us get the right pattern. A selector has an inbuilt `remove_namespaces()` function to make sure that the entire document is scanned and all the namespaces are removed. Make sure before using it whether we want some of these namespaces to be part of the pattern or not. The following is example of `remove_namespaces()` function:

```
In [17] sel.remove_namespaces()

sel.xpath("//link")
```

Now that we have more understanding about the selectors, let's modify the same old news spider that we built previously:

```
>>>from scrapy.spider import BaseSpider

>>>class NewsSpider(BaseSpider):

>>>    name = "news"

>>>    allowed_domains = ["nytimes.com"]

>>>    start_URLss = [

>>>        'http://www.nytimes.com/'

>>>    ]
```

```
>>>def parse(self, response):
>>>     sel = Selector(response)
>>>         sites = sel.xpath('//ul/li')
>>>         for site in sites:
>>>             title = site.xpath('a/text()').extract()
>>>             link = site.xpath('a/@href').extract()
>>>             desc = site.xpath('text()').extract()
>>>             print title, link, desc
```

Here, we mainly modified the parse method, which is one of the core of our spider. This spider can now crawl through the entire page, but we do a more structured parsing of the title, description, and URLs.

Now, let's write a more robust crawler using all the capabilities of Scrapy.

Items

Until now, we were just printing the crawled content on `stdout` or dumping it in a file. A better way to do this is to define `items.py` every time we write a crawler. The advantage of doing this is that we can consume these items in our parse method, and this can also give us output in any data format, such as XML, JSON, or CSV. So, if you go back to your old crawler, the items class will have a function like this:

```
>>>fromscrapy.item import Item, Field
>>>class NewsItem(scrapy.Item):
>>>     # define the fields for your item here like:
>>>     # name = scrapy.Field()
>>>     pass
```

Now, let's make it like the following by adding different fields:

```
>>>from scrapy.item import Item, Field
>>>class NewsItem(Item):
>>>     title = Field()
>>>     link = Field()
>>>     desc = Field()
```

Here, we added `field()` to `title`, `link`, and `desc`. Once we have a field in place, our spider parse method can be modified to `parse_news_item`, where instead dumping the parsed fields to a file now it can be consumed by an item object.

A Rule method is a way of specifying what kind of URL needs to be crawled after the current one. A Rule method provides `SgmlLinkExtractor`, which is a way of defining the URL pattern that needs to be extracted from the crawled page. A Rule method also provides a `callback` method, which is typically a pointer for a spider to look for the parsing method, which in this case is `parse_news_item`. In case we have a different way to parse, then we can have multiple rules and parse methods. A Rule method also has a Boolean parameter to follow, which specifies whether links should be followed by each response extracted with this rule. If the callback is None, follow defaults to *True*: otherwise, it default to *False*.

One important point to note is that the Rule method does not use parse. This is because the name of the default callback method is `parse()` and if we use it, we are actually overriding it, and that can stop the functionality of the crawl spider. Now, let's jump on to the following code to understand the preceding methods and parameters:

```
>>>from scrapy.contrib.spiders import CrawlSpider, Rule
>>>from scrapy.contrib.linkextractors.sgml import SgmlLinkExtractor
>>>from scrapy.selector import Selector
>>>from scrapy.item import NewsItem
>>>class NewsSpider(CrawlSpider):
>>>     name = 'news'
>>>     allowed_domains = ['news.google.com']
>>>     start_urls = ['https://news.google.com']
>>>     rules = (
>>>         # Extract links matching cnn.com
>>>         Rule(SgmlLinkExtractor(allow=('cnn.com', ), deny=(http://
edition.cnn.com/', ))),
>>>        # Extract links matching 'news.google.com'
>>>        Rule(SgmlLinkExtractor(allow=('news.google.com', )),
callback='parse_news_item'),
>>>     )
>>>     def parse_news_item(self, response):
>>>         sel = Selector(response)
>>>         item = NewsItem()
>>>         item['title'] = sel.xpath('//title/text()').extract()
>>>         item[topic] = sel.xpath('/div[@class="topic"]').extract()
>>>         item['desc'] = sel.xpath('//td//text()').extract()
>>>         return item
```

The Sitemap spider

If the site provides `sitemap.xml`, then a better way to crawl the site is to use `SiteMapSpider` instead.

Here, given `sitemap.xml`, the spider parses the URLs provided by the site itself. This is a more polite way of crawling and good practice:

```
>>>from scrapy.contrib.spiders import SitemapSpider
>>>class MySpider(SitemapSpider):
>>>     sitemap_URLss = ['http://www.example.com/sitemap.xml']
>>>     sitemap_rules = [('/electronics/', 'parse_electronics'), ('/apparel/', 'parse_apparel'),]
>>>     def 'parse_electronics'(self, response):
>>>         # you need to create an item for electronics,
>>>         return
>>>     def 'parse_apparel'(self, response):
>>>         #you need to create an item for apparel
>>>         return
```

In the preceding code, we wrote one parse method for each product category. It's a great use case if you want to build a price aggregator/comparator. You might want to parse different attributes for different products, for example, for electronics, you might want to scrape the tech specification, accessory, and price; while for apparels, you are more concerned about the size and color of the item. Try your hand at using one of the retailer sites and use shell to get the patterns to scrape the size, color, and price of different items. If you do this, you should be in a good shape to write your first industry standard spider.

In some cases, you want to crawl a website that needs you to log in before you can enter some parts of the website. Now, Scrapy has a workaround that too. They implemented `FormRequest`, which is more of a **POST** call to the HTTP server and gets the response. Let's have a deeper look into the following spider code:

```
>>>class LoginSpider(BaseSpider):
>>>     name = 'example.com'
>>>     start_URLss = ['http://www.example.com/users/login.php']
>>>     def parse(self, response):
>>>         return [FormRequest.from_response(response, formdata={'username': 'john', 'password': 'secret'}, callback=self.after_login)]
>>>     def after_login(self, response):
>>>         # check login succeed before going on
```

```
>>>         if "authentication failed" in response.body:
>>>             self.log("Login failed", level=log.ERROR)
>>>           return
```

For a website that requires just the username and password without any captcha, the preceding code should work just by adding the specific login details. This is the part of the parse method since you need to log in the first page in the most of the cases. Once you log in, you can write your own `after_login` callback method with items and other details.

The item pipeline

Let's talk about some more item postprocessing. Scrapy provides a way to define a pipeline for items as well, where you can define the kind of post processing an item has to go through. This is a very methodical and good program design.

We need to build our own item pipeline if we want to post process scraped items, such as removing noise and case conversion, and in other cases, where we want to derive some values from the object, for example, to calculate the age from DOB or to calculate the discount price from the original price. In the end, we might want to dump the item separately into a file.

The way to achieve this will be as follows:

1. We need to define an item pipeline in `setting.py`:

   ```
   ITEM_PIPELINES = {
       'myproject.pipeline.CleanPipeline': 300,
       'myproject.pipeline.AgePipeline': 500,
       'myproject.pipeline.DuplicatesPipeline: 700,
       'myproject.pipeline.JsonWriterPipeline': 800,
   }
   ```

2. Let's write a class to clean the items:

   ```
   >>>from scrapy.exceptions import Item
   >>>import datetime
   >>>import datetime
   >>>class AgePipeline(object):
   >>>    def process_item(self, item, spider):
   >>>        if item['DOB']:
   >>>            item['Age'] = (datetime.datetime.
   strptime(item['DOB'], '%d-%m-%y').date()-datetime.datetime.
   strptime('currentdate, '%d-%m-%y').date()).days/365
   >>>            return item
   ```

3. We need to derive the age from DOB. We used Python's date functions to achieve this:

```
>>>from scrapy import signals
>>>from scrapy.exceptions import Item
>>>class DuplicatesPipeline(object):
>>>    def __init__(self):
>>>        self.ids_seen = set()
>>>    def process_item(self, item, spider):
>>>        if item['id'] in self.ids_seen:
>>>            raise DropItem("Duplicate item found: %s" % item)
>>>        else:
>>>            self.ids_seen.add(item['id'])
>>>            return item
```

4. We also need to remove the duplicates. Python has the `set()` data structure that only contains unique values, we can create a pipline `DuplicatesPipeline.py` like below using Scrapy :

```
>>>from scrapy import signals
>>>from scrapy.exceptions import Item
>>>class DuplicatesPipeline(object):
>>>    def __init__(self):
>>>        self.ids_seen = set()
>>>    def process_item(self, item, spider):
>>>        if item['id'] in self.ids_seen:
>>>            raise DropItem("Duplicate item found: %s" % item)
>>>        else:
>>>            self.ids_seen.add(item['id'])
>>>            return item
```

5. Let's finally write the item in the JSON file using `JsonWriterPipeline.py` pipeline:

```
>>>import json
>>>class JsonWriterPipeline(object):
>>>    def __init__(self):
>>>        self.file = open('items.txt', 'wb')
>>>    def process_item(self, item, spider):
>>>        line = json.dumps(dict(item)) + "\n"
>>>        self.file.write(line)
>>>        return item
```

External references

I encourage you to follow some simple spiders and try building some cool applications using these spiders. I would also like you to look at the following links for reference:

- `http://doc.scrapy.org/en/latest/intro/tutorial.html`
- `http://doc.scrapy.org/en/latest/intro/overview.html`

Summary

In this chapter, you learned about another great Python library and now, you don't need help from anybody for your data needs. You learned how you can write a very sophisticated crawling system, and now you know how to write a focused spider. In this chapter, we saw how to abstract the item logic from the main system and how to write some specific spider for the most common use cases. We know some of the most common settings that need to be taken care of in order to implement our own spider and we wrote some complex parse methods that can be reused. We understand selectors very well and know a hands-on way of figuring out what kind of elements we want for specific item attributes, and we also went through Firebug to get more of a practical understanding of selectors. Last but not least, very importantly, make sure that you follow the security guidelines of the websites you crawl.

In the next chapter, we will explore some essential Python libraries that can be used for natural language processing and machine learning.

8
Using NLTK with Other Python Libraries

In this chapter, we will explore some of the backbone libraries of Python for machine learning and natural language processing. Until now, we have used NLTK, Scikit, and genism, which had very abstract functions, and were very specific to the task in hand. Most of statistical NLP is heavily based on the vector space model, which in turn depends on basic linear algebra covered by NumPy. Also many NLP tasks, such as POS or NER tagging, are really classifiers in disguise. Some of the libraries we will discuss are heavily used in all these tasks.

The idea behind this chapter is to give you a quick overview of some the most fundamental Python libraries. This will help us understand more than just the data structure, design, and math behind some of the coolest libraries, such as NLTK and Scikit, which we have discussed in the previous chapters.

We will look at the following four libraries. I have tried to keep it short, but I highly encourage you to read in more detail about these libraries if you want Python to be a one-stop solution to most of your data science needs.

- NumPy (Numeric Python)
- SciPy (Scientific Python)
- Pandas (Data manipulation)
- Matplotlib (Visualization)

NumPy

NumPy is a Python library for dealing with numerical operations, and it's really fast. NumPy provides some of the highly optimized data structures, such as ndarrays. NumPy has many functions specially designed and optimized to perform some of the most common numeric operations. This is one of the reasons NLTK, scikit-learn, pandas, and other libraries use NumPy as a base to implement some of the algorithms. This section will give you a brief summary with running examples of NumPy. This will not just help us understand the fundamental data structures beneath NLTK and other libraries, but also give us the ability to customize some of these functionalities to our needs.

Let's start with discussion on ndarrays, how they can be used as matrices, and how easy and efficient it is to deal with matrices in NumPy.

ndarray

An ndarray is an array object that represents a multidimensional, homogeneous array of fixed-size items.

We will start with building an ndarray using an ordinary Python list:

```
>>>x=[1,2,5,7,3,11,14,25]
>>>import numpy as np
>>>np_arr=np.array(x)
>>>np_arr
```

As you can see, this is a linear 1D array. The real power of Numpy comes with 2D arrays. Let's move to 2D arrays. We will create one using a Python list of lists.

```
>>>arr=[[1,2],[13,4],[33,78]]
>>>np_2darr= np.array(arr)
>>>type(np_2darr)
numpy.ndarray
```

Indexing

The ndarray is indexed more like Python containers. NumPy provides a slicing method to get different views of the ndarray.

```
>>>np_2darr.tolist()
[[1, 2], [13, 4], [33, 78]]
>>>np_2darr[:]
array([[1, 2], [13,  4], [33, 78]])
>>>np_2darr[:2]
array([[1, 2], [13, 4]])
>>>np_2darr[:1]
array([[1, 2]])
>>>np_2darr[2]
array([33, 78])
>>>     np_2darr[2][0]
>>>33
>>>     np_2darr[:-1]
array([[1, 2], [13, 4]])
```

Basic operations

NumPy also has some other operations that can be used in various numeric processing. In this example, we want to get an array with values ranging from 0 to 10 with a step size of `0.1`. This is typically required for any optimization routine. Some of the most common libraries, such as Scikit and NLTK, actually use these NumPy functions.

```
>>>>import numpy as np
>>>>np.arange(0.0, 1.0, 0.1)
array([ 0. ,  0.1,  0.2,  0.3,  0.4,  0.5,  0.6,  0.7,  0.8,  0.9,  1]
```

We can do something like this, and generate a array with all ones and all zeros:

```
>>>np.ones([2, 4])
array([[1., 1., 1., 1.], [1., 1., 1., 1.]])
>>>np.zeros([3,4])
array([[0., 0., 0., 0.], [0., 0., 0., 0.], [0., 0., 0., 0.]])
```

Wow!

If you have done higher school math, you know that we need all these matrixes to perform many algebraic operations. And guess what, most of the Python machine learning libraries also do that!

```
>>>np.linspace(0, 2, 10)
array([    0.,     0.22222222,     0.44444444,     0.66666667,
0.88888889,     1.11111111,     1.33333333,     1.55555556,     1.77777778,
2,     ])
```

The `linespace` function returns number samples which are evenly spaced, calculated over the interval from the start and end values. In the given example we were trying to get 10 sample in the range of 0 to 2.

Similarly, we can do this at the log scale. The function here is:

```
>>>np.logspace(0,1)
array([    1.,     1.04811313,     1.09854114,     1.1513954,     7.90604321,
8.28642773,     8.68511374,     9.10298178,     9.54095476,     10.,     ])
```

You can still execute Python's help function to get more details about the parameter and the return values.

```
>>>help(np.logspace)
Help on function logspace in module NumPy.core.function_base:


logspace(start, stop, num=50, endpoint=True, base=10.0)
    Return numbers spaced evenly on a log scale.


    In linear space, the sequence starts at ``base ** start``
    (`base` to the power of `start`) and ends with ``base ** stop``
```

```
(see `endpoint` below).

Parameters
----------
start : float
```

So we have to provide the start and end and the number of samples we want on the scale; in this case, we also have to provide a base.

Extracting data from an array

We can do all sorts of manipulation and filtering on the ndarrays. Let's start with a new Ndarray, `A`:

```
>>>A = array([[0, 0, 0], [0, 1, 2], [0, 2, 4], [0, 3, 6]])


>>>B = np.array([n for n in range n for n in range(4)])
>>>B
array([0, 1, 2, 3])
```

We can do this kind of conditional operation, and it's very elegant. We can observe this in the following example:

```
>>>less_than_3 = B<3 # we are filtering the items that are less than 3.
>>>less_than_3
array([ True,  True,  True, False], dtype=bool)
>>>B[less_than_3]
array([0, 1, 2])
```

We can also assign a value to all these values, as follows:

```
>>>B[less_than_3] = 0
>>>: B
array([0, 0, 0, 3])
```

There is a way to get the diagonal of the given matrix. Let's get the diagonal for our matrix A:

```
>>>np.diag(A)
array([0, 1, 4])
```

Complex matrix operations

One of the common matrix operations is element-wise multiplication, where we will multiply one element of a matrix by an element of another matrix. The shape of the resultant matrix will be same as the input matrix, for example:

```
>>>A = np.array([[1,2],[3,4]])
>>>A * A
array([[ 1,  4], [ 9, 16]])
```

However, we can't perform the following operation, which will throw an error when executed:

```
>>>A * B
---------------------------------------------------------------
-----------------
ValueError Traceback (most recent call last)
<ipython-input-53-e2f71f566704> in <module>()
----> 1 A*B
```

ValueError: Operands could not be broadcast together with shapes (2,2) (4,).

Simply, the numbers of columns of the first operand have to match the number of rows in the second operand for matrix multiplication to work.

Let's do the dot product, which is the backbone of many optimization and algebraic operations. I still feel doing this in a traditional environment was not very efficient. Let's see how easy it is in NumPy, and how super-efficient it is in terms of memory.

```
>>>np.dot(A, A)
array([[ 7, 10], [15, 22]])
```

We can do operations like add, subtract, and transpose, as shown in the following example:

```
>>>A - A
array([[0, 0], [0, 0]])
>>>A + A
array([[2, 4], [6, 8]])
>>>np.transpose(A)
array([[1, 3], [2, 4]])
>>>>A
array([[1, 2], [2, 3]])
```

The same transpose operations can be performed using an alternative operation, such as this:

```
>>>A.T
array([[1, 3], [2, 4]])
```

We can also cast these ndarrays into a matrix and perform matrix operations, as shown in the following example:

```
>>>M = np.matrix(A)
>>>M
matrix([[1, 2], [3, 4]])
>>> np.conjugate(M)
matrix([[1, 2], [3, 4]])
>>> np.invert(M)
matrix([[-2, -3], [-4, -5]])
```

We can perform all sorts of complex matrix operations with NumPy, and they are pretty simple to use too! Please have a look at documentation for more information on NumPy.

Let's switch back to some of the common mathematics operations, such as min, max, mean, and standard deviation, for the given array elements. We have generated the normal distributed random numbers. Let's see how these things can be applied there:

```
>>>N = np.random.randn(1,10)
>>>N
array([[  0.59238571,   -0.22224549,   0.6753678,   0.48092087,
-0.37402105,   -0.54067842,   0.11445297,   -0.02483442,
-0.83847935,   0.03480181,   ]])
>>>N.mean()
-0.010232957191371551
>>>N.std()
0.47295594072935421
```

This was an example demonstrating how NumPy can be used to perform simple mathematic and algebraic operations of finding out the mean and standard deviation of a set of numbers.

Reshaping and stacking

In case of some of the numeric, algebraic operations we do need to change the shape of resultant matrix based on the input matrices. NumPy has some of the easiest ways of reshaping and stacking the matrix in whichever way you want.

```
>>>A
array([[1, 2], [3, 4]])
```

If we want a flat matrix, we just need to reshape it using NumPy's `reshape()` function:

```
>>>>(r, c) = A.shape  # r is rows and c is columns
>>>>r,c
(2L, 2L)
>>>>A.reshape((1, r * c))
array([[1, 2, 3, 4]])
```

This kind of reshaping is required in many algebraic operations. To flatten the ndarray, we can use the `flatten()` function:

```
>>>A.flatten()
array([1, 2, 3, 4])
```

There is a function to repeat the same elements of the given array. We need to just specify the number of times we want the element to repeat. To repeat the ndarray, we can use the `repeat()` function:

```
>>>np.repeat(A, 2)
array([1, 1, 2, 2, 3, 3, 4, 4])
>>>>A
array([[1, 2],[3, 4]])
```

In the preceding example, each element is repeated twice in sequence. A similar function known as `tile()` is used for for repeating the matrix, and is shown here:

```
>>>np.tile(A, 4)
array([[1, 2, 1, 2, 1, 2, 1, 2], [3, 4, 3, 4, 3, 4, 3, 4]])
```

There are also ways to add a row or a column to the matrix. If we want to add a row, we use the `concatenate()` function shown here:

```
>>>B = np.array([[5, 6]])
>>>np.concatenate((A, B), axis=0)
array([[1, 2], [3, 4], [5, 6]])
```

This can also be achieved using the `Vstack()` function shown here:

```
>>>np.vstack((A, B))
array([[1, 2], [3, 4], [5, 6]])
```

Also, if you want to add a column, you can use the `concatenate()` function in the following manner:

```
>>>np.concatenate((A, B.T), axis=1)
array([[1, 2, 5], [3, 4, 6]])
```

Alternatively, the `hstack()` function can be used to add columns. This is used very similarly to the `vstack()` function in the example shown above.

Random numbers

Random number generation is also used across many tasks involving NLP and machine learning tasks. Let's see how easy it is to get a random sample:

```
>>>from numpy import random
>>>#uniform random number from [0,1]
>>>random.rand(2, 5)
array([[ 0.82787406, 0.21619509, 0.24551583, 0.91357419, 0.39644969], [
0.91684427, 0.34859763, 0.87096617, 0.31916835, 0.09999382]])
```

There is one more function called `random.randn()`, which generates normally distributed random numbers in the given range. So, in the following example, we want random numbers between `2` and `5`.

```
>>>>random.randn(2, 5)
array([[-0.59998393, -0.98022613, -0.52050449, 0.73075943, -0.62518516],
[ 1.00288355, -0.89613323,  0.59240039, -0.89803825, 0.11106479]])
```

This is achieved by using the function `random.randn(2,5)`.

SciPy

Scientific Python or SciPy is a framework built on top of NumPy and ndarray and was essentially developed for advanced scientific operations such as optimization, integration, algebraic operations, and Fourier transforms.

The concept was to efficiently use ndarrays to provide some of these common scientific algorithms in a memory-efficient manner. Because of NumPy and SciPy, we are in a state where we can focus on writing libraries such as scikit-learn and NLTK, which focus on domain-specific problems, while NumPy / SciPy do the heavy lifting for us. We will give you a brief overview of the data structures and common operations provided in SciPy. We get the details of some of the black-box libraries, such as scikit-learn and understand what goes on behind the scenes.

```
>>>import scipy as sp
```

This is how you import SciPy. I am using `sp` as an alias but you can import everything.

Let's start with something we are more familiar with. Let's see how integration can be achieved here, using the `quad()` function.

```
>>>from scipy.integrate import quad, dblquad, tplquad
>>>def f(x):
>>>     return x
>>>x_lower == 0 # the lower limit of x
>>>x_upper == 1 # the upper limit of x
>>>val, abserr = = quad(f, x_lower, x_upper)
>>>print val,abserr
>>> 0.5 , 5.55111512313e-15
```

If we integrate the `x`, it will be x2/2, which is `0.5`. There are other scientific functions, such as these:

- Interpolation (`scipy.interpolate`)
- Fourier transforms (`scipy.fftpack`)
- Signal processing (`scipy.signal`)

But we will focus on only linear algebra and optimization because these are more relevant in the context of machine learning and NLP.

Linear algebra

The linear algebra module contains a lot of matrix-related functions. Probably the best contribution of SciPy is sparse matrix (CSR matrix), which is used heavily in other packages for manipulation of matrices.

SciPy provides one of the best ways of storing sparse matrices and doing data manipulation on them. It also provides some of the common operations, such as linear equation solving. It has a great way of solving eigenvalues and eigenvectors, matrix functions (for example, matrix exponentiation), and more complex operations such as decompositions (SVD). Some of these are the behind-the-scenes optimization in our ML routines. For example, SVD is the simplest form of LDA (topic modeling) that we used in *Chapter 6, Text Classification*.

The following is an example showing how the linear algebra module can be used:

```
>>>A = = sp.rand(2, 2)
>>>B = = sp.rand(2, 2)
>>>import Scipy
>>>X = = solve(A, B)
>>>from Scipy import linalg as LA
>>>X = = LA.solve(A, B)
>>>LA.dot(A, B)
```

Detailed documentation is available at `http://docs.scipy.org/doc/Scipy/reference/linalg.html`.

eigenvalues and eigenvectors

In some of the NLP and machine learning applications, we represent the documents as term document matrices. Eigenvalues and eigenvectors are typically calculated for many different mathematical formulations. Say A is our matrix, and there exists a vector v such that $Av=\lambda v$.

In this case, λ will be our eigenvalue and v will be our eigenvector. One of the most commonly used operation, the **singular value decomposition** (**SVD**)will require some calculus functionality. It's quite simple to achieve this in SciPy.

```
>>>evals = LA.eigvals(A)
>>>evals
array([-0.32153198+0.j, 1.40510412+0.j])
```

And eigen vectors are as follows:

```
>>>evals, evect = LA.eig(A)
```

We can perform other matrix operations, such as inverse, transpose, and determinant:

```
>>>LA.inv(A)
array([[-1.24454719, 1.97474827], [ 1.84807676, -1.15387236]])
>>>LA.det(A)
-0.4517859060209965
```

The sparse matrix

In a real-world scenario, when we use a typical matrix, most of the elements of this matrix are zeroes. It is highly inefficient to go over all these non-zero elements for any matrix operation. As a solution to this kind of problem, a sparse matrix format has been introduced, with the simple idea of storing only non-zero items.

A matrix in which most of the elements are non-zeroes is called a dense matrix, and the matrix in which most of the elements are zeroes is called a sparse matrix.

A matrix is typically a 2D array with an index of row and column will provide the value of the element. Now there are different ways in which we can store sparse matrices:

- **DOK (Dictionary of keys)**: Here, we store the dictionary with keys in the format (*row*, *col*) and the values are stored as dictionary values.
- **LOL (list of list)**: Here, we provide one list per row, with only an index of the non-zero elements.
- **COL (Coordinate list)**: Here, a list (*row, col, value*) is stored as a list.
- **CRS/CSR (Compressed row Storage)**: A CSR matrix reads values first by column; a row index is stored for each value, and column pointers are stored (*val*, *row_ind*, *col_ptr*). Here, *val* is an array of the non-zero values of the matrix, *row_ind* represents the row indices corresponding to the values, and *col_ptr* is the list of *val* indexes where each column starts. The name is based on the fact that column index information is compressed relative to the COO format. This format is efficient for arithmetic operations, column slicing, and matrix-vector products.

See `http://docs.scipy.org/doc/Scipy-0.15.1/reference/generated/Scipy.sparse.csr_matrix.html` for more information.

- **CSC (sparse column)**: This is similar to CSR, except that the values are read first by column; a row index is stored for each value, and column pointers are stored. In otherwords, CSC is (*val*, *row_ind*, *col_ptr*).

Have a look at the documentation at:

`http://docs.scipy.org/doc/Scipy-0.15.1/reference/generated/Scipy.sparse.csc_matrix.html`

Let's have some hands-on experience with CSR matrix manipulation. We have a sparse matrix `A`:

```
>>>from scipy import sparse as s
>>>A = array([[1,0,0],[0,2,0],[0,0,3]])
>>>A
array([[1, 0, 0], [0, 2, 0], [0, 0, 3]])
>>>from scipy import sparse as sp
>>>C = = sp.csr_matrix(A);
>>>C
<3x3 sparse matrix of type '<type 'NumPy.int32'>'
    with 3 stored elements in Compressed Sparse Row format>
```

If you read very carefully, the CSR matrix stored just three elements. Let's see what it stored:

```
>>>C.toarray()
array([[1, 0, 0], [0, 2, 0], [0, 0, 3]])
>>>C * C.todense()
matrix([[1, 0, 0], [0, 4, 0], [0, 0, 9]])
```

This is exactly what we are looking for. Without going over all the zeroes, we still got the same results with the CSR matrix.

```
>>>dot(C, C).todense()
```

Optimization

I hope you understand that every time we have built a classifier or a tagger in the background, all these are some sort of optimization routine. Let's have some basic understanding about the function provided in SciPy. We will start with getting a minima of the given polynomial. Let's jump to one of the example snippets of the optimization routine provided by SciPy.

```
>>>def f(x):
>>>    returnx          return x**2-4
>>>optimize.fmin_bfgs(f,0)
Optimization terminated successfully.
         Current function value: -4.000000
         Iterations: 0
```

```
        Function evaluations: 3
        Gradient evaluations: 1
array([0])
```

Here, the first argument is the function you want the minima of, and the second is the initial guess for the minima. In this example, we already knew that zero will be the minima. To get more details, use the function `help()`, as shown here:

```
>>>help(optimize.fmin_bfgs)
Help on function fmin_bfgs in module Scipy.optimize.optimize:


fmin_bfgs(f, x0, fprime=None, args=(), gtol=1e-05, norm=inf,
epsilon=1.4901161193847656e-08, maxiter=None, full_output=0, disp=1,
retall=0, callback=None)
    Minimize a function using the BFGS algorithm.


    Parameters
    ----------
    f : callable f(x,*args)
        Objective function to be minimized.
    x0 : ndarray
        Initial guess.
>>>from scipy import optimize
            optimize.fsolve(f, 0.2)
array([ 0.46943096])


>>>def f1 def f1(x,y):
>>>     return x ** 2+  y ** 2 - 4
>>>optimize.fsolve(f1, 0, 0)
array([ 0.])
```

To summarize, we now have enough knowledge about SciPy's most basic data structures, and some of the most common optimization techniques. The intention was to motivate you to not just run black-box machine learning or natural language processing, but to go beyond that and get the mathematical context about the ML algorithms you are using and also have a look at the source code and try to understand it.

Implementing this will not just help your understanding about the algorithm, but also allow you to optimize/customize the implementation to your need.

pandas

Let's talk about pandas, which is one of the most exciting Python libraries, especially for people who love **R** and want to play around with the data in a more vectorized manner. We will devote this part of the chapter only to pandas; we will discuss some basic data manipulation and handling in pandas frames.

Reading data

Let's start with one of the most important tasks in any data analysis to parse the data from a CSV/other file.

I am using `https://archive.ics.uci.edu/ml/machine-learning-databases/adult/adult.data and attributes`

`https://archive.ics.uci.edu/ml/machine-learning-databases/iris/iris.names`

Feel free to use any other CSV file.

To begin, please download the data to your local storage from the preceding links, and load it into a pandas data-frame, as shown here:

```
>>>import pandas as pd
>>># Please provide the absolute path of the input file
>>>data = pd.read_csv("PATH\\iris.data.txt",header=0")
>>>data.head()
```

	4.9	**3.0**	**1.4**	**0.2**	**Iris-setosa**
0	4.7	3.2	1.3	0.2	Iris-setosa
1	4.6	3.1	1.5	0.2	Iris-setosa
2	5.0	3.6	1.4	0.2	Iris-setosa

This will read a CSV file and store it in a DataFrame. Now, there are many options you have while reading a CSV file. One of the problems is that we read the first line of the data in this DataFrame as a header; to use the actual header, we need to set the option header to None, and pass a list of names as column names. If we already have the header in perfect form in the CSV, we don't need to worry about the header as pandas, by default, assumes the first line to be the header. The header 0 in the preceding code is actually the row number that will be treated as the header.

So let's use the same data, and add the header into the frame:

```
>>>data = pd.read_csv("PATH\\iris.data.txt", names=["sepal length",
"sepal width", "petal length", "petal width", "Cat"], header=None)
>>>data.head()
```

	sepal length	sepal width	petal length	petal width	Cat
0	4.9	3.0	1.4	0.2	Iris-setosa
1	4.7	3.2	1.3	0.2	Iris-setosa
2	4.6	3.1	1.5	0.2	Iris-setosa

This has created temporary column names for the frame so that, in case you have headers in the file as a first row, you can drop the header option, and pandas will detect the first row of the file as the header. The other common options are Sep/Delimiter, where you want to specify the delimiter used to separate the columns. There are at least 20 different options available, which can be used to optimize the way we read and cleanse our data, for example removing Na's, removing blank lines, and indexing based on the specific column. Please have a look at the different type of files:

- `read_csv`: reading a CSV file.
- `read_excel`: reading a XLS file.
- `read_hdf`: reading a HDFS file.
- `read_sql`: reading a SQL file.
- `read_json`: reading a JSON file.

These can be the substitutes for all the different parsing methods we discussed in *Chapter 2, Text Wrangling and Cleansing*. The same numbers of options are available to write files too.

Now let's see the power of pandas frames. If you are an R programmer, you would love to see the summary and header option we have in R.

```
>>>data.describe()
```

The `describe()` function will give you a brief summary of each column and the unique values.

```
>>>sepal_len_cnt=data['sepal length'].value_counts()
>>>sepal_len_cnt


5.0     10
6.3      9
6.7      8
5.7      8
5.1      8
dtype: int64
>>>data['Iris-setosa'].value_counts()
Iris-versicolor    50
Iris-virginica     50
Iris-setosa        48
dtype: int64
```

Again for R lovers, we are now dealing with vectors, so that we can look for each value of the column by using something like this:

```
>>>data['Iris-setosa'] == 'Iris-setosa'
0      True
1      True


147     False
148     False
Name: Iris-setosa, Length: 149, dtype: bool
```

Now we can filter the DataFrame in place. Here the setosa will have only entries related to `Iris-setosa`.

```
>>>sntsosa=data[data['Cat'] == 'Iris-setosa']
>>>sntsosa[:5]
```

This is our typical SQL `Group By` function. We have all kinds of aggregate functions as well.

You can browse through the following link to look at Dow Jones data: `https://archive.ics.uci.edu/ml/machine-learning-databases/00312/`

Series data

Pandas also have a neat way of indexing by date, and then using the frame for all sorts of time series kind of analysis. The best part is that once we have indexed the data by date some of the most painful operations on the dates will be a command away from us. Let's take a look at series data, such as stock price data for a few stocks, and how the values of the opening and closing stock change weekly.

```
>>>import pandas as pd
>>>stockdata = pd.read_csv("dow_jones_index.data",parse_dates=['date'],
index_col=['date'], nrows=100)
>>>>stockdata.head()
```

date	quarter	stock	open	high	low	close	volume	percent_change_price
01/07/2011	1	AA	$15.82	$16.72	$15.78	$16.42	239655616	3.79267
01/14/2011	1	AA	$16.71	$16.71	$15.64	$15.97	242963398	-4.42849
01/21/2011	1	AA	$16.19	$16.38	$15.60	$15.79	138428495	-2.47066

```
>>>max(stockdata['volume'])
   1453438639
>>>max(stockdata['percent_change_price'])
   7.62173999999999991
>>>stockdata.index
<class 'pandas.tseries.index.DatetimeIndex'>
[2011-01-07, ..., 2011-01-28]
Length: 100, Freq: None, Timezone: None
>>>stockdata.index.day
array([ 7, 14, 21, 28, 4, 11, 18, 25, 4, 11, 18, 25, 7, 14, 21, 28, 4,11,
18, 25, 4, 11, 18, 25, 7, 14, 21, 28, 4])
```

The preceding command gives the day of the week for each date.

```
>>>stockdata.index.month
```

The preceding command lists different values by month.

```
>>>stockdata.index.year
```

The preceding command lists different values by year.

You can aggregate the data using a resample with whatever aggregation you want. It could be sum, mean, median, min, or max.

```
>>>import numpy as np
>>>stockdata.resample('M', how=np.sum)
```

Column transformation

Say we want to filter out columns or to add a column. We can achieve this by just by providing a list of columns as an argument to `axis 1`. We can drop the columns from a data frame like this:

```
>>>stockdata.drop(["percent_change_volume_over_last_wk"],axis=1)
```

Let's filter out some of the unwanted columns, and work with a limited set of columns. We can create a new `DataFrame` like this:

```
>>>stockdata_new = pd.DataFrame(stockdata, columns=["stock","open","high"
,"low","close","volume"])
>>>stockdata_new.head()
```

We can also run R-like operations on the columns. Say I want to rename the columns. I can do something like this:

```
>>>stockdata["previous_weeks_volume"] = 0
```

This will change all the values in the column to 0. We can do it conditionally and create derived variables in place.

Noisy data

A typical day in the life of a data scientist starts with data cleaning. Removing noise, cleaning unwanted files, making sure that date formats are correct, ignoring noisy records, and dealing with missing values. Typically, the biggest chunk of time is spent on data cleansing rather than on any other activity.

In a real-world scenario, the data is messy in most cases, and we have to deal with missing values, null values, Na's, and other formatting issues. So one of the major features of any data library is to deal with all these problems and address them in an efficient way. pandas provide some amazing features to deal with some of these problems.

```
>>>stockdata.head()
>>>stockdata.dropna().head(2)
```

Using the preceding command we get rid of all the Na's from our data.

date	quarter	Stock	open	high	low	close	volume	percent_change_price
01/14/2011	1	AA	$16.71	$16.71	$15.64	$15.97	242963398	-4.42849
01/21/2011	1	AA	$16.19	$16.38	$15.60	$15.79	138428495	-2.47066
01/28/2011	1	AA	$15.87	$16.63	$15.82	$16.13	151379173	1.63831

You also noticed that we have a $ symbol in front of the value, which makes the numeric operation hard. Let's get rid of that, as it will give us noisy results otherwise (for example. $43.86 is not among the top values here).

```
>>>import numpy
>>>stockdata_new.open.describe()
count          100
unique          99
top         $43.86
freq          2
Name: open, dtype: object
```

We can perform some operations on two columns, and derive a new variable out of this:

```
>>>stockdata_new.open = stockdata_new.open.str.replace('$', '').convert_
objects(convert_numeric=True)
>>>stockdata_new.close = stockdata_new.close.str.replace('$', '').
convert_objects(convert_numeric=True)
>>>(stockdata_new.close - stockdata_new.open).convert_objects(convert_
numeric=True)
```

```
>>>stockdata_new.open.describe()
count     100.000000
mean       51.286800
std        32.154889
min        13.710000
25%        17.705000
50%        46.040000
75%        72.527500
max       106.900000
Name: open, dtype: float64
```

We can also perform some arithmetic operations, and create new variables out of it.

```
>>>stockdata_new['newopen'] = stockdata_new.open.apply(lambda x: 0.8 * x)
>>>stockdata_new.newopen.head(5)
```

We can filter the data on the value of a column in this way too. For example, let's filter out a dataset for one of the companies among all those that we have the stock values for.

```
>>>stockAA = stockdata_new.query('stock=="AA"')
>>>stockAA.head()
```

To summarize, we have seen some useful functions related to data reading, cleaning, manipulation, and aggregation in this section of pandas. In the next section, will try to use some of these data frames to generate visualization out of this data.

matplotlib

matplotlib is a very popular visualization library written in Python. We will cover some of the most commonly used visualizations. Let's start by importing the library:

```
>>>import matplotlib
>>>import matplotlib.pyplot as plt
>>>import numpy
```

We will use the same running data set from the Dow Jones index for some of the visualizations now. We already have stock data for company "AA". Let's make one more frame for a new company CSCO, and plot some of these:

```
>>>stockCSCO = stockdata_new.query('stock=="CSCO"')
>>>stockCSCO.head()
>>>from matplotlib import figure
>>>plt.figure()
>>>plt.scatter(stockdata_new.index.date,stockdata_new.volume)
>>>plt.xlabel('day') # added the name of the x axis
>>>plt.ylabel('stock close value') # add label to y-axis
>>>plt.title('title') # add the title to your graph
>>>plt.savefig("matplot1.jpg")  # savefig in local
```

You can also save the figure as a JPEG/PNG file. This can be done using the `savefig()` function shown here:

```
>>>plt.savefig("matplot1.jpg")
```

Subplot

Subplot is the best way to layout your plots. This works as a canvas, where we can add not just one plot but multiple plots. In this example, we have tried to put four plots with the parameters numrow, numcol which will define the canvas and the next argument in the plot number.

```
>>>plt.subplot(2, 2, 1)
>>>plt.plot(stockAA.index.weekofyear, stockAA.open, 'r--')
>>>plt.subplot(2, 2, 2)
>>>plt.plot(stockCSCO.index.weekofyear, stockCSCO.open, 'g-*')
>>>plt.subplot(2, 2, 3)
>>>plt.plot(stockAA.index.weekofyear, stockAA.open, 'g--')
>>>plt.subplot(2, 2, 4)
>>>plt.plot(stockCSCO.index.weekofyear, stockCSCO.open, 'r-*')
>>>plt.subplot(2, 2, 3)
```

```
>>>plt.plot(x, y, 'g--')
>>>plt.subplot(2, 2, 4)
>>>plt.plot(x, y, 'r-*')
>>>fig.savefig("matplot2.png")
```

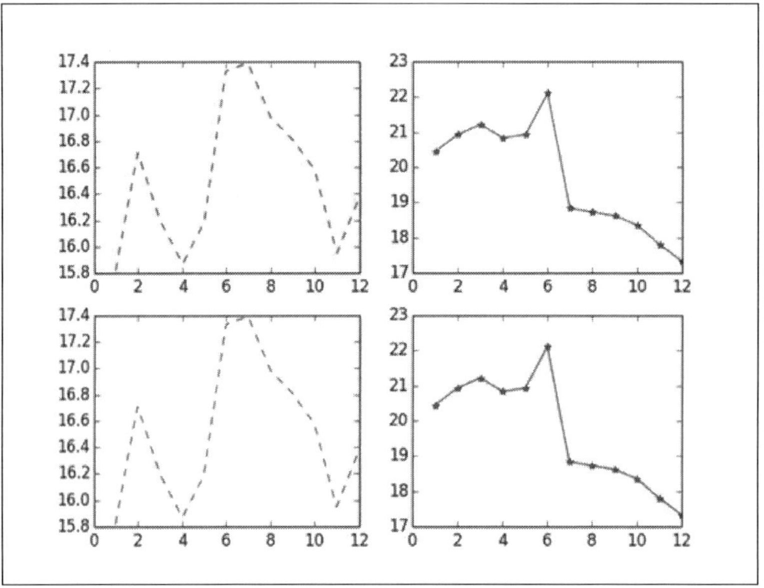

We can do something more elegant for plotting many plots at one go!

```
>>>fig, axes = plt.subplots(nrows=1, ncols=2)
>>>for ax in axes:
>>>      ax.plot(x, y, 'r')
>>>      ax.set_xlabel('x')
>>>      ax.set_ylabel('y')
>>>      ax.set_title('title');
```

As you case see, there are ways to code a lot more like in typical Python to handle different aspects of the plots you want to achieve.

Adding an axis

We can add an axis to the figure by using `addaxis()`. By adding an axis to the figure, we can define our own drawing area. `addaxis()` takes the following arguments:

```
*rect* [*left*, *bottom*, *width*, *height*]
>>>fig = plt.figure()
>>>axes = fig.add_axes([0.1, 0.1, 0.8, 0.8]) # left, bottom, width,
height (range 0 to 1)
>>>axes.plot(x, y, 'r')
```

Let' plot some of the most commonly used type of plots. The great thing is that most of the parameters, such as title and label, still work in the same way. Only the kind of plot will change.

If you want to add an x label, a y label, and a title with the axis; the commands are as follows:

```
>>>fig = plt.figure()
>>>ax = fig.add_axes([0.1, 0.1, 0.8, 0.8])
>>>ax.plot(stockAA.index.weekofyear,stockAA.open,label="AA")
>>>ax.plot(stockAA.index.weekofyear,stockCSCO.open,label="CSCO")
>>>ax.set_xlabel('weekofyear')
>>>ax.set_ylabel('stock value')
>>>ax.set_title('Weekly change in stock price')
>>>ax.legend(loc=2); # upper left corner
>>>plt.savefig("matplot3.jpg")
```

Try writing the preceding code and observe the output!

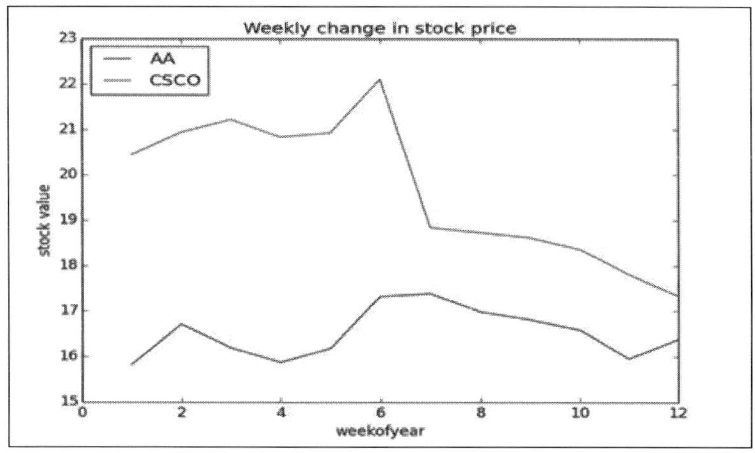

A scatter plot

One of the simplest forms of plotting is to plot the y-axis point for different x-axis values. In the following example, we have tried to capture the variation of the stock price weekly in a scatter plot:

```
>>>import matplotlib.pyplot as plt
>>>plt.scatter(stockAA.index.weekofyear,stockAA.open)
>>>plt.savefig("matplot4.jpg")
>>>plt.close()
```

A bar plot

Intuitively, the distribution of the y axis is shown against the x axis in the following bar chart. In the following example, we have used a bar plot to display data on a graph.

```
>>>n = 12
>>>X = np.arange(n)
>>>Y1 = np.random.uniform(0.5, 1.0, n)
>>>Y2 = np.random.uniform(0.5, 1.0, n)
>>>plt.bar(X, +Y1, facecolor='#9999ff', edgecolor='white')
>>>plt.bar(X, -Y2, facecolor='#ff9999', edgecolor='white')
```

3D plots

We can also build some spectacular 3D visualizations in matplotlib. The following example shows how one can create a 3D plot using matplotlib:

```
>>>from mpl_toolkits.mplot3d import Axes3D
>>>fig = plt.figure()
>>>ax = Axes3D(fig)
>>>X = np.arange(-4, 4, 0.25)
>>>Y = np.arange(-4, 4, 0.25)
>>>X, Y = np.meshgrid(X, Y)
>>>R = np.sqrt(X**2+ + Y**2)
>>>Z = np.sin(R)
>>>ax.plot_surface(X, Y, Z, rstride=1, cstride=1, cmap='hot')
```

External references

I like to encourage readers to go over some of the following links for more details about the individual libraries, and for more resources:

- `http://www.NumPy.org/`
- `http://www.Scipy.org/`
- `http://pandas.pydata.org/`
- `http://matplotlib.org/`

Summary

This chapter was a brief summary of some of the most fundamental libraries of Python that do a lot of heavy lifting for us when we deal with text and other data. NumPy helps us in dealing with numeric operations and the kind of data structure required for some of these. SciPy has many scientific operations that are used in various Python libraries. We learned how to use these functions and data structures.

We have also touched upon pandas, which is a very efficient library for data manipulation, and has been getting a lot of mileage in recent times. Finally, we gave you a quick view of one of Python's most commonly used visualization libraries, matplotlib.

In the next chapter, we will focus on social media. We will see how to capture data from some of the common social networks and produce meaningful insights around social media.

9
Social Media Mining in Python

This chapter is all about social media. Though it's not directly related to NLTK / NLP, social data is also a very rich source of unstructured text data. So, as NLP enthusiasts, we should have the skill to play with social data. We will try to explore how to gather relevant data from some of the most popular social media platforms. We will cover how to gather data from Twitter, Facebook, and so on using Python APIs. We will explore some of the most common use cases in the context of social media mining, such as trending topics, sentiment analysis, and so on.

You already learned a lot of topics under the concepts of natural language processing and machine learning in the last few chapters. We will try to build some of the applications around social data in this chapter. We will also provide you with some of the best practices to deal with social data, and look at social data from the context of graph visualization.

There is a graph that underlies social media and most of the graph-based problems can be formulated as information flow problems and finding out the busiest node in the graph. Some of the problems such as trending topics, influencer detection, and sentiment analysis are examples of these. Let's take some of these use cases, and build some cool applications around these social networks.

By the end of this chapter,:

- You should be able to collect data from any social media using APIs.
- You will also learn to formulate the data in a structured format and how to build some amazing applications.
- Lastly, we will be able to visualize and gain meaningful insight out of social media.

Data collection

The most important objective of this chapter is to gather data across some of the most common social networks. We will look mainly at Twitter and Facebook and try to give you enough details about the API and how to effectively use them to get relevant data. We will also talk about the data dictionary for scrapped data, and how we can build some cool apps using some of the stuff we learned so far.

Twitter

We will start with one of the most popular and open social media that is completely public. This means that practically, you can gather entire Twitter stream, which is payable, while you can capture one percent of the stream for free. In the context of business, Twitter is a very rich resource of information such as public sentiments and emerging topics.

Let's get directly to face the main challenge of getting the tweets relevant to your use case.

The following is the repository of many Twitter libraries. These libraries are not verified by Twitter, but run on the Twitter API.

`https://dev.twitter.com/overview/api/twitter-libraries`

There are more than 10 Python libraries there. So pick and choose the one you like. I generally use Tweepy and we will use it to run the examples in this book. Most of the libraries are wrappers around the Twitter API, and the parameters and signatures of all these are roughly the same.

The simplest way to install Tweepy is to install it using `pip`:

```
$ pip install tweepy
```

The hard way is to build it from source. The GitHub link to Tweepy is: `https://github.com/tweepy/tweepy`.

To get Tweepy to work, you have to create a developer account with Twitter and get the access tokens for your application. Once you complete this, you will get your credentials and below these, the keys. Go through `https://apps.twitter.com/app/new` for registration and access tokens. The following snapshot shows the access tokens:

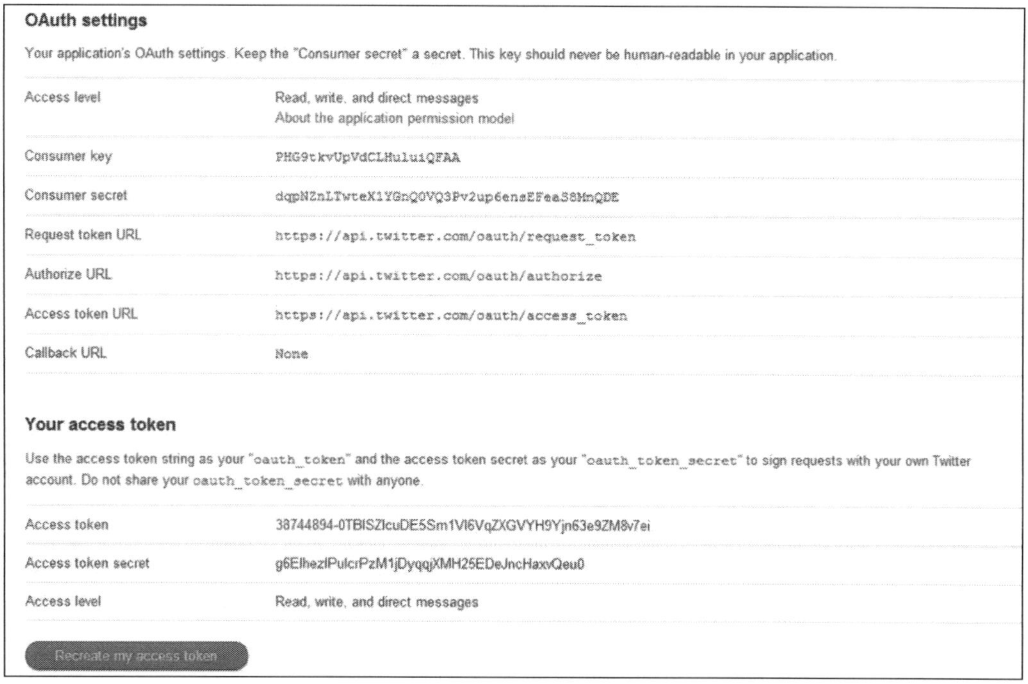

OAuth settings

Your application's OAuth settings. Keep the "Consumer secret" a secret. This key should never be human-readable in your application.

Access level	Read, write, and direct messages About the application permission model
Consumer key	PHG9tkvUpVdCLHuluiQFAA
Consumer secret	dqpNZnLTwteX1YGnQ0VQ3Pv2up6ensEFeaS8MnQDE
Request token URL	https://api.twitter.com/oauth/request_token
Authorize URL	https://api.twitter.com/oauth/authorize
Access token URL	https://api.twitter.com/oauth/access_token
Callback URL	None

Your access token

Use the access token string as your "oauth_token" and the access token secret as your "oauth_token_secret" to sign requests with your own Twitter account. Do not share your oauth_token_secret with anyone.

Access token	38744894-0TBISZlcuDE5Sm1Vl6VqZXGVYH9Yjn63e9ZM8v7ei
Access token secret	g6ElhezlPulcrPzM1jDyqqjXMH25EDeJncHaxvQeu0
Access level	Read, write, and direct messages

Recreate my access token

We will start with a very simple example to gather data using Twitter's streaming API. We are using Tweepy to capture the Twitter stream to gather all the tweets related to the given keywords:

```
tweetdump.py
>>>from tweepy.streaming import StreamListener
>>>from tweepy import OAuthHandler
>>>from tweepy import Stream
>>>import sys
>>>consumer_key = 'ABCD012XXXXXXXXx'
>>>consumer_secret = 'xyz123xxxxxxxxxxxxx'
>>>access_token = '000000-ABCDXXXXXXXXXXX'
>>>access_token_secret ='XXXXXXXXXgaw2KYz0VcqCO0F3U4'
>>>class StdOutListener(StreamListener):
>>>     def on_data(self, data):
>>>         with open(sys.argv[1],'a') as tf:
>>>             tf.write(data)
>>>         return
```

```
>>>     def on_error(self, status):
>>>         print(status)
>>>if __name__ == '__main__':
>>>     l = StdOutListener()
>>>     auth = OAuthHandler(consumer_key, consumer_secret)
>>>     auth.set_access_token(access_token, access_token_secret)
>>>     stream = Stream(auth, l)
>>>     stream.filter(track=['Apple watch'])
```

In the preceding code, we used the same code given in the example of Tweepy, with a little modification. This is an example where we use the streaming API of Twitter, where we track **Apple Watch**. Twitter's streaming API provides you the facility of conducting a search on the actual Twitter stream and you can consume a maximum of one percent of the stream using this API.

In the preceding code, the main parts that you need to understand are the first and last four lines. In the initial lines, we are specifying the access tokens and other keys that we generated in the previous section. In the last four lines, we create a listener to consume the stream. In the last line, we use `stream.filter` to filter Twitter for keywords that we have put in the track. We can specify multiple keywords here. This will result in all the tweets that contain the term Apple Watch for our running example.

In the following example, we will load the tweets we have collected, and have a look at the tweet structure and how to extract meaningful information from it. A typical tweet JSON structure looks similar to:


```
{
"created_at":"Wed May 13 04:51:24 +0000 2015",
"id":598349803924369408,
"id_str":"598349803924369408",
"text":"Google launches its first Apple Watch app with News & Weather
http:\/\/t.co\/o1XMBmhnH2",
"source":"\u003ca href=\"http:\/\/ifttt.com\" rel=\"nofollow\"\
u003eIFTTT\u003c\/a\u003e",
"truncated":false,
"in_reply_to_status_id":null,
"user":{
"id":1461337266,
"id_str":"1461337266",
```

```
"name":"vestihitech \u0430\u0432\u0442\u043e\u043c\u0430\u0442",
"screen_name":"vestihitecha",
"location":"",
"followers_count":20,
"friends_count":1,
"listed_count":4,
""statuses_count":7442,
"created_at":"Mon May 27 05:51:27 +0000 2013",
"utc_offset":14400,
},
,
"geo":{ "latitude" : 51.4514285, "longitude"=-0.99
}
"place":"Reading, UK",
"contributors":null,
"retweet_count":0,
"favorite_count":0,
"entities":{
"hashtags":["apple watch", "google"
],
"trends":[
],
"urls":[
{
"url":"http:\/\/t.co\/o1XMBmhnH2",
"expanded_url":"http:\/\/ift.tt\/1HfqhCe",
"display_url":"ift.tt\/1HfqhCe",
"indices":[
66,
88
]
}
],
"user_mentions":[
],
"symbols":[
```

```
]
},
"favorited":false,
"retweeted":false,
"possibly_sensitive":false,
"filter_level":"low",
"lang":"en",
"timestamp_ms":"1431492684714"
}
]
```


Data extraction

Some of the most commonly used fields of interest in data extraction are:

- `text`: This is the content of the tweet provided by the user
- `user`: These are some of the main attributes about the user, such as username, location, and photos
- `Place`: This is where the tweets are posted, and also the geo coordinates
- `Entities`: Effectively, these are the hashtags and topics that a user attaches to his / her tweets

Every attribute in the previous figure can be a good use case for some of the social mining exercises done in practice. Let's jump onto the topic of how we can get to these attributes and convert them to a more readable form, or how we can process some of these:

Source: `tweetinfo.py`

```
>>>import json
>>>import sys
>>>tweets = json.loads(open(sys.argv[1]).read())

>>>tweet_texts = [ tweet['text']\
                              for tweet in tweets ]
>>>tweet_source = [tweet ['source'] for tweet in tweets]
>>>tweet_geo = [tweet['geo'] for tweet in tweets]
```

```
>>>tweet_locations = [tweet['place'] for tweet in tweets]
>>>hashtags = [ hashtag['text'] for tweet in tweets for hashtag in
tweet['entities']['hashtags'] ]
>>>print tweet_texts
>>>print tweet_locations
>>>print tweet_geo
>>>print hashtags
```

The output of the preceding code will give you, as expected, four lists in which all the tweet content is in `tweet_texts` and the location of the tweets and hashtags.

In the code, we are just loading a JSON output generated using `json.loads()`. I would recommend you to use an online tool such as Json Parser (`http://json.parser.online.fr/`) to get an idea of what your JSON looks like and what are its attributes (key and value).

Next, if you look, there are different levels in the JSON, where some of the attributes such as text have a direct value, while some of them have more nested information. This is the reason you see, where when we are looking at hashtags, we have to iterate one more level, while in case of text, we just fetch the values. Since our file actually has a list of tweets, we have to iterate that list to get all the tweets, while each tweet object will look like the example tweet structure.

Trending topics

Now, if we look for trending topics in this kind of a setup. One of the simplest ways to find them could be to look for frequency distribution of words across tweets. We already have a list of `tweet_text` that contains the tweets:

```
>>>import nltk
>>>from nltk import word_tokenize,sent_tokenize
>>>from nltk import FreqDist
>>>tweets_tokens = []

>>>for tweet in tweet_text:
>>>     tweets_tokens.append(word_tokenize(tweet))
```

```
>>>Topic_distribution = nltk.FreqDist(tweets_tokens)
>>>Freq_dist_nltk.plot(50, cumulative=False)
```

One other more complex way of doing this could be the use of the part of speech tagger that you learned in *Chapter 3, Part of Speech Tagging*. The theory is that most of the time, topics will be nouns or entities. So, the same exercise can be done like this. In the preceding code, we read every tweet and tokenize it, and then use POS as a filter to only select nouns as topics:

```
>>>import nltk
>>>Topics = []
>>>for tweet in tweet_text:
>>>     tagged = nltk.pos_tag(word_tokenize(tweet))
>>>     Topics_token = [word for word,pos in ] in tagged if pos in
['NN','NNP']
>>>     print Topics_token
```

If we want to see a much cooler example, we can gather tweets across time and then generate plots. This will give us a very clear idea of the trending topics. For example, the data we are looking for is "Apple Watch". This word should peak on the day when Apple launched Apple Watch and the day they started selling it. However, it will be interesting to see what kind of topics emerged apart from those, and how they trended over time.

Geovisualization

One of the other common application of social media is geo-based visualization. In the tweet structure, we saw attributes named geo, longitude, and latitude. Once you have access to these values, it is very easy to use some of the common visualization libraries, such as **D3**, to come up with something like this:

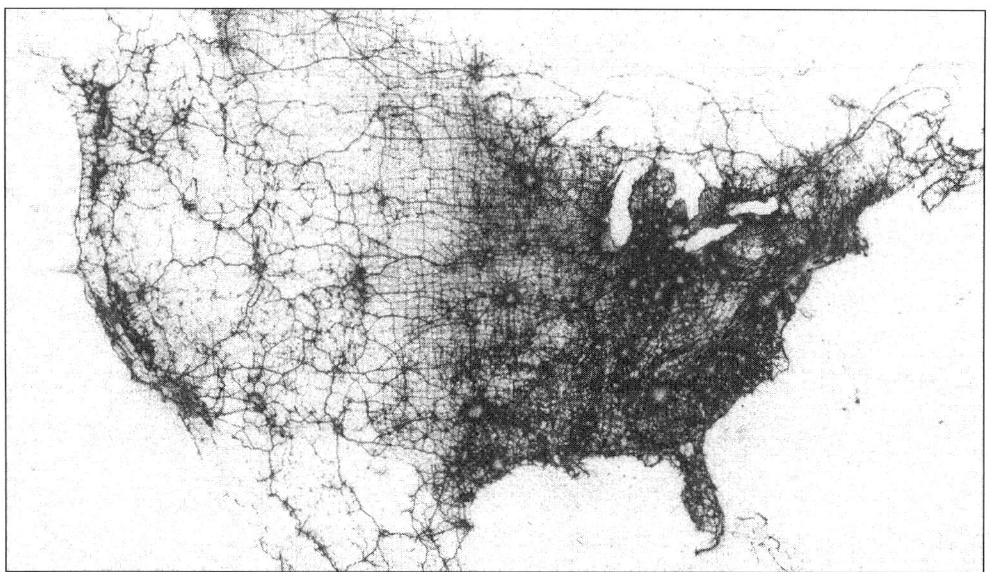

This is just an example of what we can achieve with these kind of visualizations; this was the visualization of a tweet in the U.S. We can clearly see the areas of increased intensity in eastern places such as New York. Now, a similar analysis done by a company on the customers can give a clear insight about which are some of the most popular places liked by our customer base. We can text mine these tweets for sentiment, and then we can infer insights about customers as to in which states they are not happy with the company and so on.

Influencers detection

Detection of important nodes in the social graph that has a lot of importance is another great problem in the context of social graphs. So, if we have millions of tweets streaming about our company, then one important use case would be to gather the most influential customers in the social media, and then target them for branding, marketing, or improving customer engagement.

In the case of Twitter, this goes back to the graph theory and concept of PageRank, where in a given node, if the ratio of outdegree and indegree is high, then that node is an influencer. This is very intuitive since people who have more followers than the number of people they follow are typically, influencers. One company, **KLOUT,** (`https://klout.com/`) has been focusing on a similar problem. Let's write a very basic and intuitive algorithm to calculate Klout's score:

```
>>>klout_scores = [ (tweet['user']['followers_count]/ tweet['user']
['friends_count'],tweet['user']) for tweet in tweets ]
```

Some of the examples where we worked on Twitter will hold exactly the same modification of content field. We can build a trending topic example with Facebook posts. We can also visualize Facebook users and post on the **geomap** and influencer kind of use cases. In fact, in the next section, we will see a variation of this in the context of Facebook.

Facebook

Facebook is a bit more personal, and somewhat private social network. Facebook does not allow you to gather the feeds/posts of the user simply for security and privacy reasons. So, Facebook's graph API has a limited way of accessing the feeds of the given page. I would recommend you to go to `https://developers.facebook.com/docs/graph-api/using-graph-api/v2.3` for better understanding.

The next question is how to access the Graph API using Python and how to get started with it. There are many wrappers written over Facebook's API, and we will use one the most common Facebook SDK:

```
$ pip install facebook-sdk
```

You can also install it through:
`https://github.com/Pythonforfacebook/facebook-sdk.`

The next step is to get the access token for the application while Facebook treats every API call as an application. Even for this data collection step, we will pretend to be an application.

To get your token, go to:
`https://developers.facebook.com/tools/explorer.`

We are all set now! Let's start with one of the most widely used Facebook graph APIs. In this API, Facebook provides a graph-based search for pages, users, events, places, and so on. So, the process of getting to the post becomes a two-stage process, where we have to look for a specific pageid / userid related to our topic of interest, and then we will be able to access the feeds of that page. One simple use case for this kind of an exercise could be to use the official page of a company and look for customer complaints. The way to go about this is:

```
>>>import facebook
>>>import json

>>>fo = open("fdump.txt",'w')
>>>ACCESS_TOKEN = 'XXXXXXXXXXX' # https://developers.facebook.com/tools/
explorer
>>>fb = facebook.GraphAPI(ACCESS_TOKEN)
>>>company_page = "326249424068240"
>>>content = fb.get_object(company_page)
>>>fo.write(json.dumps(content))
```

The code will attach the token to the Facebook Graph API and then we will make a REST call to Facebook. The problem with this is that we have to have the ID of the given page with us beforehand. The code which will attach the token is as follows:


```
"website":"www.dimennachildrenshistorymuseum.org",
"can_post":true,
"category_list":[
{
"id":"244600818962350",
"name":"History Museum"
},
{
"id":"187751327923426",
"name":"Educational Organization"
}
],
"likes":1793,
},
```

```
"id":"326249424068240",
"category":"Museum/art gallery",
"has_added_app":false,
"talking_about_count":8,
"location":{
"city":"New York",
"zip":"10024",
"country":"United States",
"longitude":-73.974413,
"state":"NY",
"street":"170 Central Park W",
"latitude":40.779236
},
"is_community_page":false,
"username":"nyhistorykids",
"description":"The first-ever museum bringing American history to life
through the eyes of children, where kids plus history equals serious
fun! Kids of all ages can practice their History Detective skills at
the DiMenna Children's History Museum and:\n\n\u2022 discover the past
through six historic figure pavilions\n\n\u2022!",
"hours":{
""thu_1_close":"18:00"
},
"phone":"(212) 873-3400",
"link":"https://www.facebook.com/nyhistorykids",
"price_range":"$ (0-10)",
"checkins":1011,
"about":"The DiMenna Children' History Museum is the first-ever museum
bringing American history to life through the eyes of children. Visit it
inside the New-York Historical Society!",
"name":"New-York Historical Society DiMenna Children's History Museum",
"cover":{
"source":"https://scontent.xx.fbcdn.net/hphotos-xpf1/t31.0-8/s720x720/104
9166_672951706064675_339973295_o.jpg",
"cover_id":"672951706064675",
```

```
"offset_x":0,
"offset_y":54,
"id":"672951706064675"
},
"were_here_count":1011,
"is_published":true
},
```

Here, we showed a similar schema for the Facebook data as we did for Twitter, and now we can see what kind of information is required for our use case. In most of the cases, the user post, category, name, about, and likes are some of the important fields. In this example, we are showing a page of a museum, but in a more business-driven use case, a company page has a long list of posts and other useful information that can give some great insights about it.

Let's say I have a Facebook page for my organization xyz.org and I want to know about the users who complained about me on the page; this is good for a use case such as complaint classification. The way to achieve the application now is simple enough. You need to look for a set of keywords in `fdump.txt`, and it can be as complex as scoring using a text classification algorithm we learned in *Chapter 6, Text Classification*.

The other use case could be to look for a topic of interest, and then to look for the resulting pages for open posts and comments. This is exactly analogous to searching using the graph search bar on your Facebook home page. However, the power of doing this programmatically is that we can conduct these searches and then each page can be recursively parsed for use comments. The code for searching user data is as follows:

User search

```
>>>fb.request("search", {'q' : 'nitin', 'type' : 'user'})
Place based on the nearest location.
>>>fb.request("search", {'q' : 'starbucks', 'type' : 'place'})
Look for open pages.
>>>fb.request("search", {'q' : 'Stanford university', 'type' : page})
Look for event matching to the key word.
>>>fb.request("search", {'q' : 'beach party', 'type' : 'event'})
```

Once we have dumped all the relevant data into a structured format, we can apply some of the concepts we learned when we went through the topics of NLP and machine learning. Let's pick the same use case of finding posts, that will mostly be complaints on a Facebook page.

I assume that we now have the data in the following format:

Userid	FB Post
XXXX0001	The product was pathetic and I tried reaching out to your customer care, but nobody responded
XXXX002	Great work guys
XXXX003	Where can I call to get my account activated ??? Really bad service

We will go back to the same example we had in *Chapter 6, Text Classification,* where we built a text classifier to detect whether the **SMS** (text message) was spam. Similarly, we can create training data using this kind of data, where from the given set of posts, we will ask manual taggers to tag the comments that are complaints and the ones that are not. Once we have significant training data, we can build the same text classifier:

```
fb_classification.py
>>>from sklearn.feature_extraction.text import TfidfVectorizer
>>>vectorizer = TfidfVectorizer(min_df=2, ngram_range=(1, 2),  stop_
words='english',  strip_accents='unicode',  norm='l2')
>>>X_train = vectorizer.fit_transform(x_train)
>>>X_test = vectorizer.transform(x_test)

>>>from sklearn.linear_model import SGDClassifier
>>>clf = SGDClassifier(alpha=.0001, n_iter=50).fit(X_train, y_train)
>>>y_pred = clf.predict(X_test)
```

Let's assume that these three are the only samples. We can tag 1st and 3rd to be classified as complaints, while 2nd will not be a complaint. Although we will build a vectorizer of unigram and bigram in the same way, we can actually build a classifier using the same process. I ignored some of the preprocessing steps here. You can use the same process as discussed in *Chapter 6, Text Classification*. In some of the cases, it will be hard/expensive to get training data like this. In some of these cases, we can apply either an unsupervised algorithm, such as text clustering or topic modeling. The other way is to use some different dataset that is openly available and build model on that and apply it here. For example, in the same use case, we can crawl some of the customer complaints available on the Web and use that as training data for our model. This can work as a good proxy for labeled data.

Influencer friends

One other use case of social media could be finding out the most influencer in your social graph. In our case, it could be finding out a clear node that has a vast amount of inlinks and outlinks will be the influencer in the graph.

The same problem in the context of business can be finding out the most influential customers, and targeting them to market our products.

The code for the Influencer friends is as follows:

```
>>>friends = fb.get_connections("me", "friends")["data"]
>>>print friends
>>>for frd in friends:
>>>     print fb.get_connections(frd["id"],"friends")
```

Once you have a list of all your friends and mutual friends, you can create a data structure like this:

source node	destination node	link_exist
Frind 1	Frind 2	1
Frind 1	Frind 3	1
Frind 2	Frind 3	0
Frind 1	Frind 4	1

This a kind of data structure that can be used to generate a network, and is a very good way of visualizing the social graph. I used D3 here, but python also has a library called **NetworkX** (`https://networkx.github.io/`) that can be used to generate graph visualization, as shown in the following graph. To generate a visualization, you need to arrive at a adjacency matrix that can be created based on the bases of the preceding information about who is the friend of whom.

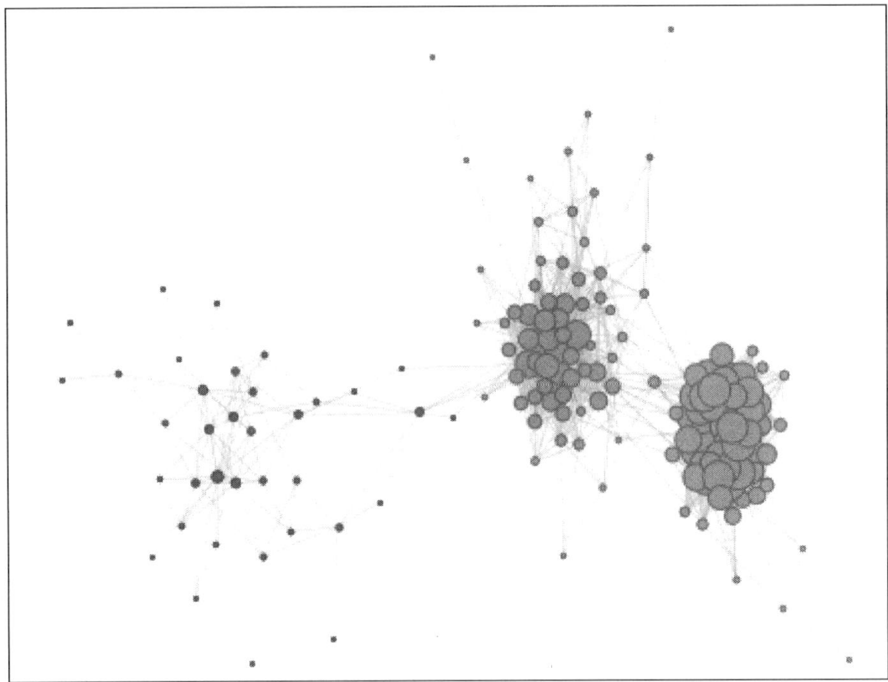

Visualization of a sample network in D3

Summary

In this chapter, we touched upon some of the most popular social networks. You learned how to get data using Python. You understood the structure and kind of attributes data has. We explored different options provided by the API.

We explored some of the most common use cases in the context of social media mining. We touched upon the use cases about trending topics, influencer detection, information flow, and so on. We visualized some of these use cases. We also applied some of the learnings from the previous chapter, where we used NLTK to get some of the topic and entity extraction, while in scikit-learn we classified some of the complaints.

In conclusion, I would suggest that you look for some of the same use cases in context of some other social networks and try to explore them. The great part of these social networks is that all of them have a data API, and most of them are open enough to do some interesting analysis. If you apply the same learning you did in this chapter, you need to understand the API, how to get the data, and then how to apply some of the concepts we learned in the previous chapters. I hope that after learning all this, you will come up with more use cases, and some interesting analysis of social media.

10
Text Mining at Scale

In this chapter, we will go back to some of the libraries we learned about in the previous chapters, but this time, we want to learn to learn how these libraries will scale up with bigdata. We assume that you have a fair bit of an idea about big data, **Hadoop** and **Hive**. We will explore how some of the Python libraries, such as NLTK, scikit-learn, and pandas can be used on a Hadoop cluster with a large amount of unstructured data.

We will cover some of the most common use cases in the context of NLP and text mining, and we will also provide a code snippet that will be helpful for you to get your job done. We will look at three major examples that can capture the vast majority of your text mining problems. We will tell you how to run NLTK at scale to perform some of the NLP tasks that we completed in the initial chapters. We will give you a few examples of some of the text classification tasks that can be done on Big Data.

One other aspect of doing machine learning and NLP at a very high scale is to understand whether the problem is parallelizable or not. We will talk in brief about some of the problems discussed in the previous chapter, and whether these problems are big data problems or not. Or in some case is it even possible to solve this using Big Data.

Since most of the libraries we learned so far are written in Python, let's deal with one of the main questions of how to get Python on Big Data (Hadoop).

By end of the chapter we like reader to have :

- Good understanding about big data related technologies such as Hadoop, Hive and how it can be done using python.
- Step by step tutorial to work with NLTK, Scikit & PySpark on Big Data.

Different ways of using Python on Hadoop

There are many ways to run a Python process on Hadoop. We will talk about some of the most popular ways through which we can run Python on Hadoop as a streaming MapReduce job, Python UDF in Hive, and Python hadoop wrappers.

Python streaming

Typically a Hadoop job has to be written in form of a map and reduce function. User has to write an implementation of map and reduce function for the given task. Commonly these mappers and reducers are implemented in JAVA. At the same time Hadoop provide streaming, you where a user can write a Python mapper and reducer function similar to Java in any other language. I am assuming that you have run a word count example using Python. We will also use the same example using NLTK later in this chapter.

In case you have not, have a look at `http://www.michael-noll.com/tutorials/writing-an-hadoop-mapreduce-program-in-python/` to know more about MapReduce in Python.

Hive/Pig UDF

Other way to use Python is by writing a **UDF** (**User Defined Function**) in Hive/Pig. The idea here is that most of the operations we are performing in NLTK are highly parallelizable. For example, POS tagging, Tokenization, Lemmatization, Stop Word removal, and NER can be highly distributable. The reason being the content of each row is independent from the other row, and we don't need any context while doing some of these operations.

So, if we have NLTK and other Python libraries on each node of the cluster, we can write a **user defined function** (**UDF**) in Python, using libraries such as NLTK and scikit. This is one of the easiest way of doing NLTK, especially for scikit on a large scale. We will give you a glimpse of both of these in this chapter.

Streaming wrappers

There is a long list of wrappers that different organizations have implemented to get Python running on the cluster. Some of them are actually quite easy to use, but all of them suffer from performance bias. I have listed some of them as follows, but you can go through the project page in case you want to know more about them:

- Hadoopy
- Pydoop
- Dumbo
- mrjob

For the exhaustive list of options available for the usage of Python on Hadoop, go through the article at `http://blog.cloudera.com/blog/2013/01/a-guide-to-python-frameworks-for-hadoop/`.

NLTK on Hadoop

We talked enough about NLTK as a library, and what are some of the most-used functions it gives us. Now, NLTK can solve many NLP problems from which many are highly parallelizable. This is the reason why we will try to use NLTK on Hadoop.

The best way of running NLTK on Hadoop is to get it installed on all the nodes of the cluster. This is probably not that difficult to achieve. There are ways in which you can do this, such as sending the resource files as a streaming argument. However, we will rather prefer the first option.

A UDF

There are a variety of ways in which we can make NLTK run on Hadoop. Let's talk about one example of using NLTK by doing tokenization in parallel using a Hive UDF.

For this use case, we have to follow these steps:

1. We have chosen a small dataset where only two columns exist. We have to create the same schema in Hive:

ID	Content
UA0001	"I tried calling you. The service was not up to the mark"
UA0002	"Can you please update my phone no"
UA0003	"Really bad experience"
UA0004	"I am looking for an iPhone"

2. Create the same schema in Hive. The following Hive script will do this for you:

   Hive script

```
CREATE TABLE $InputTableName (
ID String,
Content String
)
ROW FORMAT DELIMITED
FIELDS TERMINATED BY '\t';
```

3. Once we have the schema, essentially, we want to get something like tokens of the content in a separate column. So, we just want another column in the `$outTable` with the same schema, and the added column of tokens:

   Hive script

```
CREATE TABLE $OutTableName (
ID String,
Content String,
Tokens String
)
```

4. Now, we have the schemas ready. We have to write the UDF in Python to read the table line by line and then apply a `tokenize` method. This is very similar to what we did in *Chapter 3, Part of Speech Tagging*. This is the piece of function that is analogous to all the examples in *Chapter 3, Part of Speech Tagging*. Now, if you want to get POS tags, Lemmatization, and HTML, you just need to modify this UDF. Let's see how the UDF will look for our tokenizer:

```
>>>import sys
>>>import datetime
>>>import pickle
```

```
>>>import nltk
>>>nltk.download('punkt')
>>>for line in sys.stdin:
>>>     line = line.strip()
>>>     print>>sys.stderr, line
>>>     id, content= line.split('\t')
>>>     print>>sys.stderr,tok.tokenize(content)
>>>     tokens =nltk.word_tokenize(concat_all_text)
>>>     print '\t'.join([id,content,tokens])
```

5. Just name this UDF something like: `nltk_scoring.py`.
6. Now, we have to run the insert hive query with the `TRANSFORM` function to apply the UDF on the given content and to do tokenization and dump the tokens in the new column:

   Hive script

```
add FILE nltk_scoring.py;
add FILE english.pickle; #Adding file to DistributedCache
INSERT OVERWRITE TABLE $OutTableName
SELECT
        TRANSFORM (id, content)
    USING 'PYTHONPATH nltk_scoring.py'
    AS (id string, content string, tokens string )
FROM $InputTablename;
```

7. If you are getting an error like this, you have not installed the NLTK and NLTK data correctly:

```
raiseLookupError(resource_not_found)
LookupError:
**********************************************************************
****
  Resource u'tokenizers/punkt/english.pickle' not found.  Please
  use the NLTK Downloader to obtain the resource:  >>>
  nltk.download()
  Searched in:
    - '/home/nltk_data'
    - '/usr/share/nltk_data'
    - '/usr/local/share/nltk_data'
    - '/usr/lib/nltk_data'
    - '/usr/local/lib/nltk_data'
```

8. If you are able to run this Hive job successfully, you will get a table named `OutTableName`, that will look something like this:

ID	Content	
UA0001	"I tried calling you, The service was not up to the mark"	[" I", " tried", "calling", "you", "The", "service" "was", "not", "up", "to", "the", "mark"]
UA0002	"Can you please update my phone no"	["Can", "you", "please" "update", " my", "phone" "no"]
UA0003	"Really bad experience"	["Really"," bad" "experience"]
UA0004	"I am looking for an iphone"	["I", "am", "looking", "for", "an", "iPhone"]

Python streaming

Let's try the second option of Python streaming. We have Hadoop streaming, where we can write our own mapper and reducer functions, and then use Python streaming with `mapper.py`, as it looks quite similar to our Hive UDF. Here we are using the same example with map-reduce python streaming this will give us a option of choosing a Hive table or using a HDFS file directly. We will just go over the content of the file and tokenize it. We will not perform any reduce operation here, but for learning, I included a dummy reducer, which just dumps it. So now, we can ignore the reducer from the execution command completely.

Here is the code for the Mapper.py:

Mapper.py

```
>>>import sys
>>>import pickle
>>>import nltk
>>>for line in sys.stdin:
>>>     line = line.strip()
>>>     id, content = line.split('\t')
>>>     tokens =nltk.word_tokenize(concat_all_text)
>>>     print '\t'.join([id,content,topics])
```

Here is the code for the `Reducer.py`:

Reducer.py

```
>>>import sys
>>>import pickle
>>>import nltk
>>>for line in sys.stdin:
>>>    line = line.strip()
>>>    id, content,tokens = line.split('\t')
>>>    print '\t'.join([id,content,tokens])
```

The following is the Hadoop command to execute a Python stream:Hive script

```
hadoop jar <path>/hadoop-streaming.jar \
-D mapred.reduce.tasks=1 -file <path>/mapper.py \
-mapper <path>/mapper.py \
-file <path>/reducer.py \
-reducer <path>/reducer.py \
-input /hdfspath/infile \
-output outfile
```

Scikit-learn on Hadoop

The other important use case for big data is machine learning. Specially with Hadoop, scikit-learn is more important, as this is one of the best options we have to score a machine learning model on big data. Large-scale machine learning is currently one of the hottest topics, and doing this in a big data environment such as Hadoop is all the more important. Now, the two aspects of machine learning models are building a model on big data and to build model on a significantly large amount of data and scoring a significantly large amount of data.

To understand more, let's take the same example data we used in the previous table, where we have some customer comments. Now, we can build, let's say, a text classification mode using a significant training sample, and use some of the learnings from *Chapter 6, Text Classification* to build a Naive Bayes, SVM, or a logistic regression model on the data. While scoring, we might need to score a huge amount of data, such as customer comments. On the other hand building the model itself on big data is not possible with scikit-learn, we will require tool like spark/Mahot for that. We will take the same step-by-step approach of scoring using a pre-trained model as we did with NLTK. While building the mode on big data will be covered in the next section. For scoring using a pre-trained model specifically when we are working on a text mining kind of problem. We need two main objects (a vectorizer and modelclassifier) to be stored as a serialized pickle object.

Here, pickle is a Python module to achieve serialization by which the object will be saved in a binary state on the disk and can be consumed by loading again.

`https://docs.python.org/2/library/pickle.html`

Build an offline model using scikit on your local machine and make sure you pickle objects. For example, if I use the Naive Bayes example from *Chapter 6, Text Classification*, we need to store `vectorizer` and `clf` as pickle objects:

```
>>>vectorizer = TfidfVectorizer(sublinear_tf=True, min_df=in_min_df, 
stop_words='english', ngram_range=(1,2), max_df=in_max_df)
>>>joblib.dump(vectorizer, "vectorizer.pkl", compress=3)
>>>clf = GaussianNB().fit(X_train,y_train)
>>>joblib.dump(clf, "classifier.pkl")
```

The following are the steps for creating a output table which will have all the customer comments for the entire history:

1. Create the same schema in Hive as we did in the previous example. The following Hive script will do this for you. This table can be huge; in our case, let's assume that it contains all the customer comments about the company in the past:

   Hive script

   ```
   CREATE TABLE $InputTableName (
   ID String,
   Content String
   )
   ROW FORMAT DELIMITED
   FIELDS TERMINATED BY '\t';
   ```

2. Build an output table with the output column like the predict and probability score:

   Hive script

   ```
   CREATE TABLE $OutTableName (
   ID String,
   Content String,
   predict String,
   predict_score double
   )
   ```

3. Now, we have to load these pickle objects to the distributed cache using the `addFILE` command in Hive:

   ```
   add FILE vectorizer.pkl;
   add FILE classifier.pkl;
   ```

4. The next step is to write the Hive UDF, where we are loading these pickle objects. Now, they start behaving the same as they were on the local. Once we have the classifier and vectorizer object, we can use our test sample, which is nothing but a string, and generate the TFIDF vector out of this. The vectorizer object can be used now to predict the class as well as the probability of the class:

   Classification.py

   ```
   >>>import sys
   >>>import pickle
   >>>import sklearn
   >>>from sklearn.externals import joblib

   >>>clf = joblib.load('classifier.pkl')
   >>>vectorizer = joblib.load('vectorizer.pkl')

   >>>for line in sys.stdin:
   >>>     line = line.strip()
   >>>     id, content= line.split('\t')
   >>>     X_test = vectorizer.transform([str(content)])

   >>>     prob = clf.predict_proba(X_test)
   >>>     pred = clf.predict(X_test)
   >>>     prob_score =prob[:,1]
   >>>     print '\t'.join([id, content,pred,prob_score])
   ```

5. Once we have written the `classification.py` UDF, we have to also add this UDF to the distributed cache and then effectively, run this UDF as a `TRANSFORM` function on each and every row of the table. The Hive script for this will look like this:

   Hive script

   ```
   add FILE classification.py;


   INSERT OVERWRITE TABLE $OutTableName
   SELECT
       TRANSFORM (id, content)
       USING 'python2.7 classification.py'
       AS (id string, scorestringscore string )
   FROM $Tablename;
   ```

6. If everything goes well, then we will have the output table with the output schema as:

ID	Content	Predict	Prob_score
UA0001	"I tried calling you, The service was not up to the mark"	Complaint	0.98
UA0002	"Can you please update my phone no "	No	0.23
UA0003	"Really bad experience"	Complaint	0..97
UA0004	"I am looking for an iPhone "	No	0.01

So, our output table will have all the customer comments for the entire history, scores for whether they were complaints or not, and also a confidence score. We have choosen a Hive UDF for our example, but the similar process can be done through the Pig and Python steaming in a similar way as we did in NLTK.

This example was to give you a hands-on experience of how to score a machine learning model on Hive. In the next example, we will talk about how to build a machine learning/NLP model on big data.

PySpark

Let's go back to the same discussion we had of building a machine learning/NLP model on Hadoop and the other where we score a ML model on Hadoop. We discussed second option of scoring in depth in the last section. Instead sampling a smaller data-set and scoring let's use a larger data-set and build a large-scale machine learning model step-by-step using PySpark. I am again using the same running data with the same schema:

ID	Comment	Class
UA0001	I tried calling you, The service was not up to the mark	1
UA0002	Can you please update my phone no	0
UA0003	Really bad experience	1
UA0004	I am looking for an iPhone	0
UA0005	Can somebody help me with my password	1
UA0006	Thanks for considering my request for	0

Consider the schema for last 10 years worth of comments of the organization. Now, instead of using a small sample to build a classification model, and then using a pretrained model to score all the comments, let me give you a step-by-step example of how to build a text classification model using PySpark.

The first thing that we need to do is we need to import some of the modules. Starting with `SparkContext`, which is more of a configuration, you can provide more parameters, such as app names and others for this.

```
>>>from pyspark import SparkContext
>>>sc = SparkContext(appName="comment_classifcation")
```

For more information, go through the article at `http://spark.apache.org/docs/0.7.3/api/pyspark/pyspark.context.SparkContext-class.html`.

The next thing is reading a tab delimited text file. Reading the file should be on HDFS. This file could be huge (~Tb/Pb):

```
>>>lines = sc.textFile("testcomments.txt")
```

The lines are now a list of all the rows in the corpus:

```
>>>parts = lines.map(lambda l: l.split("\t"))
>>>corpus = parts.map(lambda row: Row(id=row[0], comment=row[1],
class=row[2]))
```

The part is a list of fields as we have each field in the line delimited on "\t".

Let's break the corpus that has [ID, comment, class (0,1)] in the different RDD objects:

```
>>>comment = corpus.map(lambda row: " " + row.comment)
>>>class_var = corpus.map(lambda row:row.class)
```

Once we have the comments, we need to do a process very similar to what we did in *Chapter 6, Text Classification*, where we used scikit to do tokenization, hash vectorizer and calculate TF, IDF, and tf-idf using a vectorizer.

The following is the snippet of how to create tokenization, term frequency, and inverse document frequency:

```
>>>from pyspark.mllib.feature import HashingTF
>>>from pyspark.mllib.feature import IDF
# https://spark.apache.org/docs/1.2.0/mllib-feature-extraction.html

>>>comment_tokenized = comment.map(lambda line: line.strip().split(" "))
>>>hashingTF = HashingTF(1000) # to select only 1000 features
>>>comment_tf = hashingTF.transform(comment_tokenized)
>>>comment_idf = IDF().fit(comment_tf)
>>>comment_tfidf = comment_idf.transform(comment_tf)
```

We will merge the class with the `tfidf` RDD like this:

```
>>>finaldata = class_var.zip(comment_tfidf)
```

We will do a typical test, and train sampling:

```
>>>train, test = finaldata.randomSplit([0.8, 0.2], seed=0)
```

Let's perform the main classification commands, which are quite similar to scikit. We are using a logistic regression, which is widely used classifier. The `pyspark.mllib` provides you with a variety of algorithms.

For more information on `pyspark.mllib` visit `https://spark.apache.org/docs/latest/api/python/pyspark.mllib.html`

The following is an example of Naive bayes classifier:

```
>>>from pyspark.mllib.regression import LabeledPoint
>>>from pyspark.mllib.classification import NaiveBayes
>>>train_rdd = train.map(lambda t: LabeledPoint(t[0], t[1]))
>>>test_rdd = test.map(lambda t: LabeledPoint(t[0], t[1]))
>>>nb = NaiveBayes.train(train_rdd,lambda = 1.0)
>>>nb_output = test_rdd.map(lambda point: (NB.predict(point.features),
point.label))
>>>print nb_output
```

The `nb_output` command contains the final predictions for the test sample. The great thing to understand is that with just less than 50 lines, we built a snippet code for an industry-standard text classification with even petabytes of the training sample.

Summary

To summarize this chapter, our objective was to apply the concepts that we learned so far in the context of big data. In this chapter, you learned how to use some Python libraries, such as NLTK and scikit with Hadoop. We talked about scoring a machine learning model, or an NLP-based operation.

We also saw three major examples of the most-common use cases. On understanding these examples, you can apply most of the NLTK, scikit and PySpark functions.

This chapter was a quick and brief introduction to NLP and text mining on big data. This is one of the hottest topics, and each term and tool which I talked about in the example snippet could be a book in itself. I tried to give you a hacker's approach, to give you an introduction to big data and text mining on a large scale. I encourage you to read more about some of these big data technologies such as Hadoop, Hive, Pig, and Spark and try to explore some of the examples we gave in this chapter.

Index

Symbol

A

B

C

D

E

F

N

O

P

Q

R

S

T

U

V

W

X

Thank you for buying
NLTK Essentials

About Packt Publishing

Packt, pronounced 'packed', published its first book, *Mastering phpMyAdmin for Effective MySQL Management*, in April 2004, and subsequently continued to specialize in publishing highly focused books on specific technologies and solutions.

Our books and publications share the experiences of your fellow IT professionals in adapting and customizing today's systems, applications, and frameworks. Our solution-based books give you the knowledge and power to customize the software and technologies you're using to get the job done. Packt books are more specific and less general than the IT books you have seen in the past. Our unique business model allows us to bring you more focused information, giving you more of what you need to know, and less of what you don't.

Packt is a modern yet unique publishing company that focuses on producing quality, cutting-edge books for communities of developers, administrators, and newbies alike. For more information, please visit our website at `www.packtpub.com`.

About Packt Open Source

In 2010, Packt launched two new brands, Packt Open Source and Packt Enterprise, in order to continue its focus on specialization. This book is part of the Packt Open Source brand, home to books published on software built around open source licenses, and offering information to anybody from advanced developers to budding web designers. The Open Source brand also runs Packt's Open Source Royalty Scheme, by which Packt gives a royalty to each open source project about whose software a book is sold.

Writing for Packt

We welcome all inquiries from people who are interested in authoring. Book proposals should be sent to `author@packtpub.com`. If your book idea is still at an early stage and you would like to discuss it first before writing a formal book proposal, then please contact us; one of our commissioning editors will get in touch with you.

We're not just looking for published authors; if you have strong technical skills but no writing experience, our experienced editors can help you develop a writing career, or simply get some additional reward for your expertise.

Machine Learning with Spark

ISBN: 978-1-78328-851-9 Paperback: 338 pages

Create scalable machine learning applications to power a modern data-driven business using Spark

1. A practical tutorial with real-world use cases allowing you to develop your own machine learning systems with Spark.
2. Combine various techniques and models into an intelligent machine learning system.
3. Use Spark's powerful tools to load, analyze, clean, and transform your data.

NumPy Cookbook
Second Edition

ISBN: 978-1-78439-094-5 Paperback: 258 pages

Over 90 fascinating recipes to learn and perform mathematical, scientific, and engineering Python computations with NumPy

1. Perform high-performance calculations with clean and efficient NumPy code.
2. Simplify large data sets by analysing them with statistical functions.
3. A solution-based guide packed with engaging recipes to execute complex linear algebra and mathematical computations.

Please check **www.PacktPub.com** for information on our titles

Hadoop MapReduce v2 Cookbook
Second Edition

ISBN: 978-1-78328-547-1 Paperback: 322 pages

Explore the Hadoop MapReduce v2 ecosystem to gain insights from very large datasets

1. Process large and complex datasets using next generation Hadoop.
2. Install, configure, and administer MapReduce programs and learn what's new in MapReduce v2.
3. More than 90 Hadoop MapReduce recipes presented in a simple and straightforward manner, with step-by-step instructions and real-world examples.

Learning SciPy for Numerical and Scientific Computing
Second Edition

ISBN: 978-1-78398-770-2 Paperback: 188 pages

Quick solutions to complex numerical problems in physics, applied mathematics, and science with SciPy

1. Use different modules and routines from the SciPy library quickly and efficiently.
2. Create vectors and matrices and learn how to perform standard mathematical operations between them or on the respective array in a functional form.
3. A step-by-step tutorial that will help users solve research-based problems from various areas of science using Scipy.

Please check **www.PacktPub.com** for information on our titles

Printed in Great Britain
by Amazon